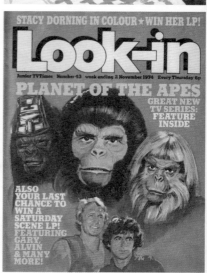

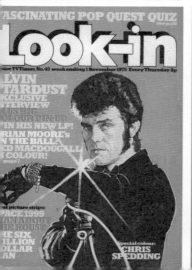

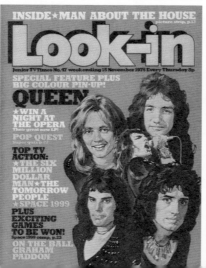

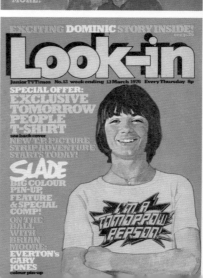

Look-in

ACKNOWLEDGEMENTS

The publishers would like to thank the team at IPC Media Ltd and DC Comics for all their help in compiling this book, particularly David Abbott and Linda Lee. Also special thanks to David Savage, Paul Moore, Jack Kibble-White and Angus Allan.

Crowther in Trouble: By arrangement with Leslie Crowther.
On the Buses: Based on the London Weekend Television series written by Ronald Wolfe and Ronald Chesney.
Catweazle © LWI Productions 1972.
Potty Time © Michael Bentine, writer and creator of the Thames Television series.
The Adventures of Black Beauty © 1974 LWI Productions.
Man About the House © 1976 John Mortimer and Brian Cooke and Thames Television.
ABBA Exclusive Official © 1978 Polar Music International AB.
The Bionic Woman © 1978 Universal City Studios.
The Bionic Woman™ Bionic™: Trademarks of and licensed by Universal City Studio Ltd.
Sapphire & Steel © P. J. Hammond 1980.

Page 124 Reprint © 2007 by DC Comics. Superman and all related names, characters and elements are trademarks of DC Comics. All Rights Reserved.

Every effort has been made to acknowledge correctly and contact the source and /or copyright holder of each picture and Carlton Books Limited apologises for any unintentional errors or omissions that will be corrected in future editions of this book.

Please do not enter any of the competitions or send money to the reader offers contained herein — it was 30-odd years ago and while we'd love a Tomorrow People T-shirt too, it's not going to happen!

Look-in

The Best of Look-in ★ Junior TVTimes ★ The Seventies

Look-in

CONTENTS

PICTURE STRIPS

Sapphire & Steel

The Power of Hecate
A young girl is possessed by the spirit of a vengeful cat-like superbeing with incredible powers of destruction.

Page 132, 136, 140

The House of the Six Locks
Jaime Sommers is given a special key, one of six that will unlock the secret vault located within a creepy old house.

The Bionic Woman
Page 100, 106, 114, 118, 122, 128

Black Beauty

Mother Dench
Can a frightening old woman tending to a sick boy really be a witch?

Page 36, 40, 48, 52, 56

The Tomorrow People

A Small Problem
When a scientist experimenting with miniaturisation accidentally shrinks himself, his garden becomes a terrifying jungle.

Page 60, 64, 68, 72, 82, 86

FUN & GAMES

La-La-La-La-La Look-in

An introduction to the legend that is *Look-in* ...

It was DJ David 'Kid' Jensen who would be first with the news every week. Sneaking into an otherwise boring TV commercial break, his excitable tones would be heard accompanying crash-zooms into picture-strips and pearly-toothed pin-ups.

'*Look-in* every week ... For explosive action with the *Bionic Woman* and the *Six Million Dollar Man*! *Look-in* every week ... For a load of fun with *Benny Hill*, *Doctor on the Go* and *Flintlock*! *Look-in* every week ... for *On The Ball*, the best in pop, super colour pin-ups! *Look-in* every week ... You'll love it!'

All to a 'La-la-la-la-la *Look-in*!' jingle strumming along in the background. No wonder a generation of fizzy sherbet-scoffing, Chopper-riding, David Essex-obsessed kids couldn't wait for Fridays to roll along. That was *Look-in* day.

The cult kids' magazine ran from 1971 to 1994. It evolved as a hybrid of two dummies for proposed publications that had been doing the rounds at the start of the seventies. One was based on the then ailing *TV21* comic, a sci-fi title with a high proportion of picture-strips based on Gerry Anderson's various television series (*Thunderbirds*, *Captain Scarlet*, etc). The other was a mooted juvenile take on the ITV TV listings magazine *TV Times*, to be titled *Magpie* in deference to Thames Television's *Blue Peter*-baiting children's show.

What we finally got was a conglomeration of the two, overseen by former *TV21* editor Alan Fennell and sporting the subtitle 'Junior TV Times'. 'There will always be something new in *Look-in*,' Fennell promised in the

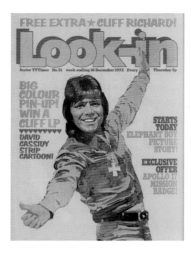

Italian-born movie poster artist Arnaldo Putzu painted most of the covers for _Look-in_, coming up with countless eye-catching classics on a weekly basis. Shown below are four original Putzu artworks from the archives, with the finished covers as they finally appeared on the newsagents' shelves shown above.

★★★

pages of issue one – and he was right. Across its run, the magazine sported the best TV-related picture-strips around, backed up with a breathless array of features and pin-ups.

A product of the television age, the magazine flourished in an era when as ordinary a programme as _Sale of the Century_ could attract 21 million viewers (as happened over Christmas 1978, believe it or not). From the very beginning, _Look-in_ ensured its pages were packed with TV faces. Issue One alone featured contributions from _Magpie_'s Tony

Bastable, _World of Sport_'s Dickie Davies (then grandly billed as 'Richard Davies'), _How_'s Fred Dinenage, TV magician David Nixon and Ed 'Stewpot' Stewart.

Every week the magazine took us behind the scenes of our favourite shows, chatted to the stars, and even enlisted some of them to write long-running columns, such as 'Stewpot's Newsdesk'. Even more exciting than that – and a key selling point in the pre-home video age – the magazine presented readers with picture-strip versions of ITV's

top-performing shows. If you felt bereft once that eponymous nag had galloped home over the end credits of _The Adventures of Black Beauty_, you could pick up the magazine and enjoy further exploits with Beauty, Jenny and all the rest of the characters from the series. Ditto for such favourites as _Man About the House_, _The Tomorrow People_, _Catweazle_, _On the Buses_, _The Bionic Woman_, _Benny Hill_ … the list goes on and on.

Angus Allan wrote more of these than anyone. Talking about the process of scripting

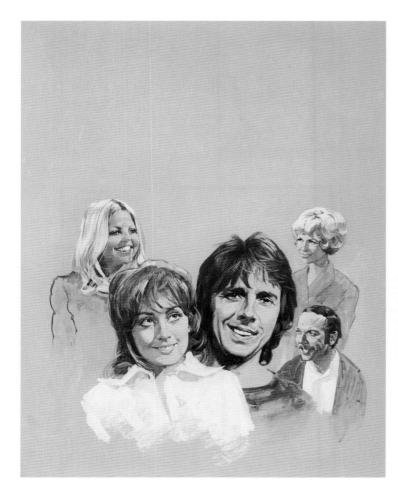

Look-in was launched in January 1971 with the full-page advert shown above in that week's issue of the parent publication *TV Times.* The picture strip below is of *Kung-Fu,* a martial arts TV Western starring David Carradine and drawn by Martin Asbury. By the 1980s Asbury was applying his dynamic style to drawing storyboards for movies including *Superman IV.*

a strip, he remembers: 'An episode would take me about an hour to write from scratch, then straight onto the typewriter. To tell the truth, I worked only two days a week – flat out without a pause from 9am until about 7pm. I haven't smoked for ten years, but back then I got through four packets a day, and a bottle of the Auld MacSpootery while I worked. The rest of the week I spent in Fleet Street pubs.'

Despite that self-deprecating description of his working methods, Allan turned out taut, exciting strips week in, week out, which remained (in the main) fairly representative of their TV counterparts. His efforts were matched by a blistering array of talented illustrators employed to realise his efforts. Mike Noble, Arthur Ranson, Martin Asbury, John M. Burns, Gerry Haylock, Bill Titcombe – all turned out sterling work for *Look-in.*

However, the artist synonymous with the magazine never actually tried his hand at picture-strips. An Italian working in a London design studio, Arnaldo Putzu initially came to prominence painting posters for movies such as *Get Carter* and *On the Buses.* By the end of its first year, *Look-in* decided to ditch photographic covers, and quickly enlisted him (more often than not) to produce those iconic, lavishly painted montages that adorned each issue and immediately set the title aside from its rivals on the news-stands.

Constantly seizing on the newest crazes, *Look-in* enjoyed a capricious relationship with pop culture, going nuts over the latest big thing (*Follyfoot*! Our Kid! Mick Robertson! The Smurfs!), before growing bored and moving on to something else.

The magazine's original designer and eventual second editor (following Alan Fennell's departure in 1975), Colin Shelbourn, describes how he chose what went in its pages:

'I was backing hunches. It was about gut feel – mine and that of others on the team. But it was easier then – there were just two channels (BBC1 and ITV), and we couldn't touch BBC as we were [attached to] *TV Times.* Therefore any reasonably decent series for children that ITV bought would have a critical mass of viewers … That was the starting point of most of what we did, but later we had to keep our eyes out for movies, so obviously *Star Wars*, *Grease* … the mega ones. Also, we had to be aware of shows that weren't designed for kids but ended up being popular with them. Like *Starsky and Hutch*.'

In its hunger for the next big thing, *Look-in* adopted a crazy kind of democracy, making for unlikely bedfellows within its pages. By the latter part of the seventies, the publication was taking punk in its stride, happily rotating covers between new-wave acts like The Jam, Blondie and Darts, and then Cliff Richard,

THE WHIRRING OF DOZENS OF COMPUTER REELS FOLLOWS – AND LIZ'S WORDS ARE WHISPERED BACK, LIKE AN ECHO …

THE BRAINS OF THE *DOMINATOR* SENSE TRUTH! BUT YOU HAVE OBVIOUS INTELLIGENCE – AND THAT CANNOT BE PERMITTED! *ALL* INTELLIGENT ONES ARE *SPIES*!

RUN, LIZ – *RUN!* THEY'RE GOING TO *KILL US!*

M. NOBLE

This *Tomorrow People* sticker, above, was a 'great free gift' in 1976. Below, the TV adverts featuring the famous 'La-la-la-la-la *Look-in*' jingle were another promotional tool used to entice new readers.

Ex-*TV21* artist Mike Noble drew many classic picture strips for *Look-in*, including one for ATV's junior sci-fi serial *Timeslip*, seen above, in 1971. *Look-in* strips including *Please, Sir!*, *Timeslip* and *Catweazle* were reprinted in *Jamin Junior*, left, a comic available from a Dutch supermarket chain in 1972.

honed or as vital. *Look-in* burned brightly throughout the Seventies and became an integral part of the pop cultural world it mirrored. Looking back on issues today is like delving into a time capsule. Flip open an edition from 1972, and you'll discover the most important things in a child's life were Marc Bolan, *Magpie* and Supermousse …

So, let's delve again. From Leslie Crowther to pop group Racey (of *Some Girls* infamy) and all points in between – courtesy of this book you hold in your hands, it's time to la-la-la-la-la look in on the best of the Seventies once more.

You'll love it!

Graham Kibble-White

Abba and The Dooleys. All were grist to the mill. More often than not, the magazine got it right – as borne out by the fact it's nigh on impossible to come across issues today still complete with those centre-spread pop pin-ups, which fast became currency for many a playground swap.

Across its life, *Look-in* spawned many rivals – *Countdown*, *TV Action*, *Target*, *Smash Hits*, *TV Tops*, *Beeb*, *Fast Forward et al* – but few ever felt as exciting, up-to-the-minute, well-

Look-in

I AM the editor of LOOK-IN—the Junior TVTimes—and I would like to welcome you to the first issue of this exciting magazine.

LOOK-IN is a new kind of publication that will keep you up-to-date with the whole television scene. Each week you will be able to see what TV programmes are on the screen in your own ITV area.

Special, colourful features about new and current TV programmes will be presented in LOOK-IN's pages, and exciting and humorous cartoon strips based on your most popular TV favourites will keep you enthralled.

I want LOOK-IN to be your publication, and throughout its pages you will be given opportunities to express your views about the magazine and television in general.

Look through the list of contents and you will see how exciting LOOK-IN is—and remember, there will always be something new in LOOK-IN.

A look at Look-in No.1

Look-in needs you!

*Y*OU have an opinion—a view about what you want to see on your screen. You know what is a good TV programme—what TV commercials you like—what TV personalities appeal to you. LOOK-IN wants to know what you want—and what you think about television.

The teletalkers service is being introduced to give you a voice in television. You can join the teletalker panel of experts by filling in the coupon below and pasting it on a postcard.

Your card will be filed on the special Teletalker Computer which, every three or four weeks, will select 50 members of the panel. You could be amongst those 50 selected Teletalkers and you will know because your name will be published in a future issue of LOOK-IN.

When your name is announced, LOOK-IN will ask you to fill in a special questionnaire.

I'm a teletalker!

AND THERE WILL BE PRIZES FOR THE SENDERS OF THE BEST RETURNED QUESTIONNAIRES.

So don't delay! Complete the coupon, paste it on a postcard and send it direct to the address shown.

NOTE: If you haven't a photograph of yourself and unfortunately no picture can be returned, use the space to give a brief description of yourself — height, colour of hair and eyes, etc.

★★ *Win yourself £1!* ★★

*R*OGER MOORE, Anita Harris, John Alderton, Charlie Drake—these great personalities are just a few of the star names who have agreed to select and introduce your letters and jokes.

'Your View' will be starting soon in LOOK-IN, and a £1 postal order — together with a special, signed photograph of the 'Your View' star —will be awarded for each item published.

So get busy today! Send letters of interest and your jokes to the address below.

Write to: 'Your View', LOOK-IN, Independent Television Publications Ltd., 247 Tottenham Court Road, London W1P OAU.

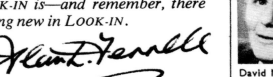

Your teletalkers coupon

NAME ....

ADDRESS ....

....

....

AGE ....

Stick your photograph here

Paste on a postcard and send to Teletalkers Service, LOOK-IN, The Junior TVTimes, 247 Tottenham Court Road, London W1P OAU.

Crowther in trouble

SUPPOSE I **OUGHT** TO GET UP. WHAT HAVE I GOT ON TODAY? OH, YES, FINAL REHEARSALS AT THE STUDIO.

THAT BOXING SKETCH WE'RE DOING, WHERE I GET KNOCKED OUT OF THE RING, SHOULD BE FUNNY...

...HOPE MASHER DAVIES KNOWS HOW TO **MISS** WITH HIS PUNCHES!

HONK-HONK!

SCREEECH!

HEY! THAT'S A STUPID THING TO DO! YOU PULLED RIGHT OUT IN FRONT OF ME!

GOOD—HE'S STOPPED! I CAN GIVE HIM A PIECE OF MY MIND!

WHO DO YOU THINK YOU'RE HONKING AT, CHUM?

WELL, IF YOU PUT ME **DOWN**, WE'LL SAY NO MORE ABOUT IT!

HUH! IF I WASN'T IN SO MUCH OF A **RUSH**, I'D HAVE SORTED HIM OUT!

AH, LESLIE—'FRAID WE'VE GOT SOME BAD NEWS. MASHER DAVIES HAS CAUGHT A COLD. WE'VE HAD TO GET A STAND-IN...

GOSH, THAT'S THE **BLOKE IN THE CAR!** HE MUST HAVE FOLLOWED ME HERE!

COME OUT FROM HIDING, LESLIE—THIS IS HORACE SMALL, MASHER'S **STAND-IN!**

IS HE NOW..! YOU MEAN HE'S WORKING FOR **US**?

RIGHT! NOW THERE'S A FEW **OFTEN** CHANGES I WANT TO MAKE IN THE SKETCH!

THAT'S BETTER! IT'S MUCH FUNNIER IF I KNOCK **HIM** OUT OF THE RING!

NOT A BAD DAY, REALLY —IT'S NOT OFTEN I WIN THE **HEAVYWEIGHT BOXING CHAMPIONSHIP!** AND THAT BLOKE HAD IT COMING!

9th January 1971 • Art: Tom Kerr • Story: Geoff Cowan

Geoff Cowan invites you to . . .

Meet the compères!

JOE BROWN—*a top pop personality with plenty of musical talent!* LES DAWSON—*that's him, in the middle of several young performers.*

KEN DODD—*provides music and laughter with a Mexican-styled song!* BOBBY BENNETT—*as he appeared in a show from an earlier series.*

"*INTRODUCING your own star-spangled spectacular— JUNIOR SHOWTIME!" And who better to make such an announcement than the programme's compère? But what does a compère do? Let's ask the producer, Mike Bevan.*

"*Most important of the Junior Showtime production are the young stars. But someone has to co-ordinate and introduce the acts. That's the job of the compère.*"

In addition to this difficult task, the compère has another important role to play—one which is not so easy to notice. He holds the show together. In other words, acts as a centre-point to keep both the performers and viewers at home happy.

Variety is what JUNIOR SHOWTIME is all about. So Mike decided that the programme should have a variety of *compères*, too; such famous stars as Ken Dodd and Billy Dainty—brilliant comedians; Joe Brown and Gerry Marsden who sing and play guitars, while Lionel Blair was

chosen for his dancing ability.

Adding to variety again, each production of JUNIOR SHOWTIME has a special theme. Remember the last show —when Les Dawson took the whole cast—and viewers— to the Zoo? There were songs, jokes and dance routines about animals, of course. Well, keep a close look out for future programmes and you will get a peep at many more subjects like 'Winter', 'London', and the 'Carnival'.

You're probably wondering why I haven't mentioned Mr. JUNIOR SHOWTIME, himself—the original resident compère—Bobby Bennett.

Yes. He appeared on some of the programmes in the present series—and he's very happy about it, too!

In fact, Bobby sums up the whole 'feel' of the show better than anything or anyone else.

"The secret of the show's success is to let the young performers have 'their heads'—and to work *with* them! It's smashing fun and it's real team production!"

Build and operate your own

![MAGPIE Studio]

YOU'RE sitting in the control room above the Magpie Studio. Before you are banks of monitor screens and a large console, by which you can keep in constant touch with the studio floor. Under your control are four cameras, coupled to monitors, a sound boom microphone, camera and boom operators, the floor manager and, of course, the presenters.

The studio is on stand-by—it's up to *you* to make it work. By using the instructions below, plus the Magpie background and other figures printed on pages 12 and 13, you can become the producer of Magpie in your own home.

You will have hours of interest and fun by lining up the model cameras before the presenters—and you can add to your model by introducing 'props' and other characters to your studio.

Watch out for next week's issue when LOOK-IN will tell you about an exciting competition involving your completed studio. You could become a guest of Magpie and appear on the TV programme.

Magpie producer Sue Turner plans the famous Thames Television series and works out the items which are suitable for presenters Susan Stranks, Tony Bastable and Pete Brady to introduce. With the LOOK-IN FREE GIFT, you can produce your own TV programme.

LOOK OUT FOR NEXT WEEK'S LOOK-IN

An additional camera, 2 camera operators, a boom operator and the MAGPIE boat. These super models are included in another fascinating FREE GIFT which will complete your Magpie studio.

Don't miss next week's

Fold and crease each section before attempting to assemble.

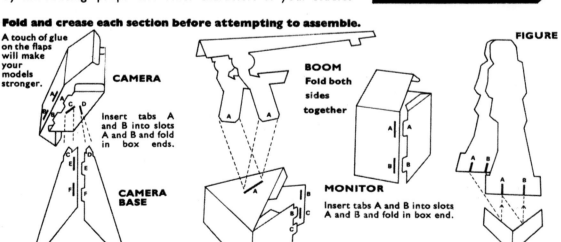

A touch of glue on the flaps will make your models stronger.

CAMERA

Insert tabs A and B into slots A and B and fold in box ends.

CAMERA BASE

Insert tabs E and F into slots E and F then join camera to base with tabs C and D

BOOM
Fold both sides together

MONITOR

Insert tabs A and B into slots A and B and fold in box end.

BOOM BASE

Insert tabs B and C into slots B and C then join boom to base with tabs A.

FIGURE

BASE

Fold both figure sides together—and slide base into slots A and B.

ROGER MOORE

Roger Moore replies...

An on-the-spot interview by LOOK-IN reporter, Geoff Cowan

Tony Curtis co-stars with Roger Moore in ATV's forthcoming television series 'The Persuaders'. Here they are seen during recent filming.

"GO AND INTERVIEW ROGER MOORE," the Editor said. **"We've had a lot of letters from LOOK-IN readers asking all sorts of questions about him. You can find out the answers . . ."**

I was more than pleased to do just that. After all, it's not every day one gets the chance of meeting the star of *Ivanhoe, Maverick* and *The Saint*—and one of TV's top actors.

I found Roger at Pinewood Studios.

"Let's sit down and talk," he invited. With that, I cast my mind back to the letters I'd been reading and let fly:

Q: Recalling your role as *Ivanhoe*—did you enjoy the part?

A: Of course! It took me back to my boyhood. It was great fun riding horses, firing bows and arrows, and sword-fighting.

Q: The *Saint* established you very much in the public eye. Were you in sympathy with the character?

A: I had to be—it was work! Seriously, though, yes. I'd read most of the Charteris books.

Q: What are your main likes?

A: Almost everything—except violence and intolerance. Oh, and I like cabbage.

Q: Surely your role as the *Saint* involved violence?

A: Not really. It was good, clean stuff. Besides, the only people who got hurt were the 'baddies'.

Q: While rehearsing for the *Saint* series, did you ever knock out anyone by mistake?

A: No. On screen, it looks better if you swing your arm when punching. But if you really want to knock out a man, you do it like this . . .

A lightning fist lanced out towards my solar plexus. It stopped inches before landing home. As I sighed with relief, I was glad that Roger disliked violence.

Q: Do you do your own stunt-work?

A: I did in the Saint. *I'd fall down a flight of forty steps—but I'd draw the line at forty-five—or falling off a horse.*

Q: What are you working on now?

A: A new series called The Persuaders. *My co-star is Tony Curtis.*

After leaving school at fifteen, Roger—son of a London policeman—entered the film world as an 'extra' and is one of the few to hit top success. In the forthcoming 'Persuaders' series he stars as the aristocratic Lord Brett Sinclair. As I spoke to him, I realised how well the casting department had done its job. Roger Moore must be the aristocrat of all TV heroes!

Striking out with Geoff Hurst

A personal interview by Richard Davies

A Bobby Moore free-kick finds Geoff Hurst's head and, next second, the ball whistles into the net. In extra time, a fierce right-foot shot hits the underside of the crossbar. This time the ball's deflected down. Is it a goal? After consultation with the linesman, the referee signals it is. In fact, it's England's winner.

But Geoff Hurst hasn't finished. A fast break down the left, a tremendous shot, the net bulges, and the hat-trick is complete. Almost immediately the final whistle signals England's greatest victory. West Germany is vanquished in the 1966 World Cup and Geoff Hurst's name enters the record book.

Reflecting on that great day, Geoff said: "Of course, I remember it with a great sense of pleasure. Before the game I was more nervous than at any other time, and when it was all over, I was exhausted.

"I just hit the ball as hard as I could . . ."

"When I scored that last goal, I just hit the ball as hard as I could. I thought if it didn't go into the net, at least it would reach the Wembley crowd behind that goal and, while the ball was retrieved, I could have a little rest. We'd played for almost *two hours* at that point!"

Last year, Geoff fought through another World Cup. In Mexico, strangely enough, it was West Germany—taking revenge—that put England out. Thinking back on that one, Geoff was less happy.

Geoff is a professional from the top of that lethal head to the tips of his deadly feet. His Dad was a 'pro' with Rochdale and Oldham, and it was an offer to play for Chelmsford that brought Mister Hurst Senior, and his family, south. So Geoff eventually joined West Ham which has been his only club.

At the moment, the club has hit hard times. But this great striker never gives less than his best. Goals are his business —and sometimes a player has to take a lot of 'stick' to score them. Geoff won't tell you this, but *I* will. It takes courage, an even temper, and an overflowing talent—and that's England's top striker, Geoff Hurst!

International Sports Special

Trying to negotiate a slippery surface at speeds of over sixty miles an hour is a very dangerous business. In World of Sport this Saturday, you can see some of the world's greatest skiers performing on packed snow, from Wengen, in Switzerland. You will be able to compare their performances with competitors in another sport, too —rallycross! Many of the top rally drivers will be taking their powerful Mini-Coopers and Capris through mud, over wet tarmac and chalk. This can be just as treacherous as speeding over snow or ice!

£1 for your star question!

Last week I asked you to write in with the question you wanted Roger Taylor to answer? Well, here are some more sports stars I will be meeting soon: Henry Cooper, Anneli Drummond-Hay (above), Mick McManus and Ron Davies. So, if you want to earn yourself £1 by having your question published on this page—together with the star's reply—hurry and write in to me now! Here is the address: Star Question, World of Sport, LOOK-IN The Junior TV Times, 247, Tottenham Court Road, W1P OAU.

Much Magic to all Readers! Geoffrey Bayldon Catweazle

GEOFFREY BAYLDON AS CATWEAZLE

PLEASE SIR!

HEDGES TAKES FIVE 'C' ON A VISIT TO THE LOCAL FARM...

ARR! IT BE A FINE IDEA TO TEACH THEY YOUNG 'UNS ABOUT FARMING, MR. HEDGES! TAKE AS LONG AS YER LIKE TO SHOW 'EM AROUND!

THAT'S VERY KIND OF YOU, FARMER!

OOOH, SIR! ARE THERE ANY LITTLE LAMBS HERE?

YEAH! AND WHERE ARE THE GORILLAS KEPT, CHIEF?

I ONLY WANNA SEE THE 'ORSES! I'LL TRY AND FIND OUT WHERE THEY ARE!

I'VE GOT A WAY WITH ANIMALS... THEY ALL LIKE ME! JUST WATCH, YOU LOT!

NOW BE CAREFUL — AND DON'T DISTURB THE CHICKENS!

AAAAGH! THE PERISHER'S 'AD ME 'AND!

SERVES YOU RIGHT FOR INTERFERING, ERIC!

YAH! I BET I CAN GET THIS 'ERE COW TO EAT A BIT OF TURNIP!

THAT'S A MANGLE WURZLE, YOU IDIOT!

S..STONE ME!

MOOO

YOU CAN'T BLAME 'IM, ERIC... IT WASN'T EVEN WRAPPED!

Geoff Cowan interviews the young stars from Timeslip
Liz & Simon

[PHOTOGRAPHS BY PAUL STOKES]

MEETING with monsters isn't the sort of thing most of us would choose to do in our spare time. But TIMESLIP adventurers Liz Skinner and Simon Randall decided that a quick trip to face the prehistoric monsters of earth's age-old past would be a good idea.

It all began when I managed to push a message through the time-barrier and tell TIMESLIP stars Cheryl Burfield and Spencer Banks to stop off and take a breather in 1971. Why? Because I thought it was about time we dug a little into their *own* pasts and found out more about these two rather remarkable people.

They agreed and soon emerged at the right time and place—within the LOOK-IN office. Eighteen-year-old Cheryl and sixteen-year-old Spencer told me it was rather strange to follow themselves in the LOOK-IN stories.

I discovered that they particularly enjoyed their adventure in the future, when our script-writer and artist dropped them into a sort of 're-evolution' of the earth. Remember the story—especially the part when they battled against the mighty Tyrannosaurus?

"I'd quite like to meet some more of those sort of creatures," Cheryl bravely announced, looking at Michael Noble's artwork. "It *was* rather exciting!"

No sooner said than done! A car took just one hour to drop us into the prehistoric world of raging monsters and flying freaks. In other words, the Crystal Palace Park Gardens where such things still exist— though, admittedly, only in stone! To Cheryl and Spencer it was like taking a trip through the time-barrier . . .

Cheryl was born in Woking, Surrey, and Spencer at Chesterfield, Derbyshire. *Cheryl* has three brothers, Gary (15), Kim (10) and Christopher (8). Twice her family has moved out to Australia and then returned. Cheryl was trained at the Professional Children's School for Drama, and has appeared in a pantomime, a West End play and in the TV programme 'Adventure Weekly'.

Spencer first took to acting during his fourth year at secondary school. Then he joined the local County Youth Theatre, and was auditioned for a television programme. Later he was offered the part as Simon in TIMESLIP.

Timeslip stars, Cheryl Burfield and Spencer Banks recall their fight with the Tyrannosaurus shown on artist Michael Noble's original drawing.

21

For a moment, even Cheryl and Spencer felt just a little nervous at meeting the monsters!

A day of chaos for Blakey!

Stan goes to France in a great new story starting next week!

MAGPIE Look-in GREAT OFFER!
Get into gear with the MAGPIE T-Shirt

Murgatroyd is flapping his wings and puffing out his chest at this great offer.

You could have an exclusive Magpie T-Shirt—just like those worn by the children in the picture—for only 75p, which includes postage and packing.

Tell mum these fabulous fun garments are British-made cotton, fully washable and run-fast. They are white, with the old bird himself and the Magpie lettering in Murgatroyd Blue emblazoned on the front. There are shirts to fit all shapes and sizes, including mum and dad, and if you act fast you could be setting the trend this Autumn with the leisure wear that everyone will be talking about.

Use the coupon on this page to tick off the number and chest sizes you want, enclose a cheque or postal order made payable to Independent Television Publications Ltd., for the correct amount (75p each shirt) and send to MAGPIE T-SHIRT OFFER, P.O. BOX 50, KETTERING, NORTHANTS.

Don't forget to fill in your name and address, and please use capital letters.

16th September 1972

CATWEAZLE

WHEN CATWEAZLE LANDS UP IN THE TWENTIETH CENTURY HE MAKES FRIENDS WITH JOE BOND, WHOSE FATHER IS A STAGE-MAGICIAN — THE GREAT BONDINI. AN ANCIENT BOOK OF BONDINI'S GIVES CATWEAZLE A FAR-FETCHED RECIPE FOR A SPELL THAT WILL TAKE HIM BACK TO HIS OWN TIME. ONE OF THE INGREDIENTS IS 'HOOT OF OWL' — BUT CATWEAZLE RECKONS HE'S FOUND THE SECRET OF COLLECTING IT...

HOOT! THOU ART *MINE* NOW, TRICKERY-BOX! HOOT, *HOOT*! I COMMAND THEE!

I MEANT NO HARM, MASTER. ALL I CRAVE IS THE HOOT OF AN OWL!

IT'S A TAPE-RECORDER — BELONGING TO THE THEATRICAL BIRD-CALL IMITATOR, EAGLE EVANS...

GAHHH! IT'S *YOU* AGAIN! PUT THAT THING DOWN BEFORE YOU *BREAK* IT, YOU OLD CLOWN!

FIE! FTTT! WHY WILL IT NOT *HOOT*?

I COME ALL THE WAY OUT HERE TO RECORD THE SONG OF A TREE-CREEPER, AND YOU BARGE IN AND RUIN EVERYTHING!

IRRITABLY, EVANS WINDS BACK AND PRESSES THE RE-PLAY BUTTON...

I DON'T KNOW WHAT YOU'RE BABBLING ABOUT! SEE HOW MUCH TAPE YOU'VE SPOILED!

HOOT! THOU ART *MINE* NOW, TRICKERY-BOX! HOOT, *HOOT*! I COMMAND THEE!

HEARING HIS OWN VOICE HAS AN ASTONISHING EFFECT ON CATWEAZLE...

EEEERK! GURRRK!

BACK AT THE THEATRE WHERE BONDINI IS PLAYING, CATWEAZLE SEEKS OUT JOE...

MMMP! URRRKK! CROAKLE!

PARDON? IS THERE ANYTHING *WRONG*?

CATWEAZLE SEEKS PEN AND PAPER. THEN...

Evil one who makes bird cries hath stolen my voice with his magic trickery-box

Next week: Catweazle's quest for mystic fire!

MAGPIE

Above: Beverly Williams takes the high-dive.   Below: Sue follows suit!

Dear Magpie,

Ours is a small village school in the North Riding of Yorkshire. We have a young ornithologists' club of twenty-five members. In the school grounds there are some big trees and we have made a bird garden. The committee organised a summer fête at Stephens House and made fifteen pounds. We will use the money to buy a feeding station, roofed feeding box and feeding table for the bird garden.

County Primary School, Gt. Smeaton.

Dear Susan and friends,

I am sending you a little poem about the astronauts. I hope you like it.

Into space oh so fast.
Watching stars floating past,
What lies beyond that distant star,
Maybe one day we'll go that far.

Into space very fast,
Watching meteors floating past,
To see the Highlands of the moon.
For man's future very soon.

Now they've landed what a thrill,
Hoping to see 'Hadley Rill',
In slow motion so it seems,
Now man's come to find his
  dreams.

Into the moon buggy off they go,
Wondering what to earth
  they'll show,
Rocks and dust and craters deep,
Perhaps even water—just a peep.

Back to earth and so they come,
Home again, a job well done,
Splashdown now, all very grand,
And once more they are on land.

Christopher Williams, Stafford.

High Dive!

Did you watch Magpie last Tuesday? If so, you'll recognise the champion diver in the picture above. She's Beverly Williams who, at just fourteen years of age, is British Ladies Diving Champion. She was giving Sue a few lessons—though, Sue seemed quite an expert!

Magpie makes a Record!

★★★★★★★★★★★★★★★★

Yes, as from last month the Magpie theme tune—which you've heard before and after every programme for more than two years—is permanently on record, and currently in the shops!

As you may have seen on the 'air', Tony and Doug went along to Decca's studios in London to help with rehearsals for the song. By the time they arrived, the backing track had already been put on to tape by Peter York (drums), Eddie Hardin (organ) and Ray Fenwick (bass guitar).

So the next step was to record the individual instruments, and then the vocalists. Tony and Doug 'donned' their headphones—to hear the backing track—and were each given an instrument to play.

Tony took up the cowbell, striking it at suitable moments with a drumstick, while Doug made music on a tambourine!

Selling at 50p (recommended retail price), the record ('Twice A Week' is on the flip side), is on the Decca label, No. F13256.

Murgatroyd's Memories

Starting this week, Magpie's own Murgatroyd looks back to memorable moments in the programme's history. See if you can remember them, too!

Murgatroyd remembers how in March 1970 Denis Wickham came to the Magpie studio at the start of a strange journey. He had decided to travel from the studio in Teddington to Brisbane in Australia. Most people who travel that distance would go the easy way, by plane. Or if they wanted to go in a different fashion, they might take a train or even drive by car. But Denis Wickham was going to travel by penny-farthing! In the picture you can see him setting off. Then just a few weeks ago, eighteen months after setting out, the news came: he had arrived in Brisbane, penny-farthing and all!

Denis Wickham sets out on his penny-farthing. But he soon finds some fellow-riders to talk to!

9th November 1974 • Art: Arthur Ranson • Story: Robin Tucek

HOW

HOW is an echo caused?

Elaine Hughes, London.

By sound being 'reflected' or bounced back from a suitable surface, like the wall of a building or a cliff. If you are less than thirty feet or so from the surface it is hard to tell the difference between the first sound—your shout, perhaps—and the echo from it. In valleys with many reflecting surfaces, it is possible to hear a whole series of echoes and this enables people to work out distances. Sound waves travel roughly a mile in five seconds. So if you shout at a suitable object and the sound comes back as an echo in ten seconds, you will know the object is a mile away.

HOW is Balsa wood made?
Mark Grove, Shrewsbury, Salop.

It comes from the Balsa tree, which is found in Central America and the northern part of South America. The wood is strong but light and the tree grows very fast, sometimes as much as fifteen feet in a single year. This results in the cells of the wood being what is called 'thin-walled'. Once the tree has been chopped down, the dead cells

become full of air, which makes balsa wood even lighter than cork.

South American Indians used balsa wood for canoes and rafts and the word 'balsa' means 'raft' in Spanish, for the Spaniards, when they came to America, in the 16th century, were very impressed by the wood's usefulness. Balsa wood is used, amongst other things, for making model planes and boats.

Left: the famous Kon Tiki raft—made of balsa wood.

HOW many satellites has Jupiter?
Paul McDonald, Middlesex.

It has twelve. Its four biggest, discovered after the invention of the telescope in the 17th century, are about the size of our Moon and can be seen through good binoculars.

HOW do we get the idea that if an ugly person looks in a mirror it would crack?

R. Ford, Devon.

This is not one of the superstitions attached to mirrors. We think it is an ancient, mean and unkind idea that has been around almost as long as mirrors have!

Did you make the Tug Boat included in the model harbour in How's *Rubbish Workshop?* If you didn't or would like to build another one, here's your chance. Follow the stage by stage instructions over the next four weeks.

THE TUG BOAT.

STAGE 1.

← ½ SAFETY-MATCHBOX STOOD ON END, WILL BE THE WHEEL-HOUSE.

SAFETY MATCHBOX LAID FLAT IN THE TRAY.

← MAIN CABIN.

THE MATERIALS YOU WILL NEED TO COMPLETE YOUR MODEL ARE:—

1 TRAY OF THE LONG FLAT TYPE OF MATCHBOX.
1½ SAFETY MATCHBOXES.
1 TOP OF SAFETY-MATCHBOX.
THE STRIKE STRIP OF A SAFETY-MATCHBOX.
1 MATCHSTICK.
1 STRIP OF BLACK PAPER ABOUT ¾" WIDE AND 13" LONG.
1 PIECE OF WHITE CARTRIDGE PAPER 6" X 4".
1 TUBE BALSA CEMENT.

TRAY OF FLAT NON-SAFETY MATCHBOX.

STAGE 2.

GLUE INTO POSITION.

THE WHEEL-HOUSE AND MAIN CABIN.

TRAY FORMING HULL OF TUG.

Look out for next week's Look-in

★ *Part three of LOOK-IN's fabulous Apollo 16 competition.* ★ *Plus: another badge offer—next week's depicts the Apollo 14 moon shot. It was chosen by the astronauts who made the epic journey. Plus: Happy Hudd time! Stewpot's Look-out includes a meeting with Roy Hudd!* ★ *Plus all your favourites!*

It's all in next week's Look-in order your copy now!

TELL ME...

Marc Bolan, pop performer extraordinary, appeared on *Magpie* recently to answer viewers' questions in the 'Tell Me' spot. LOOK-IN now presents some of the questions and answers there was no time for on the programme.

Where did you get your 1947 Gibson guitar?

From a friend who had to sell it because he needed the money. It's great—the Rolls Royce of Guitars! And there are only about half a dozen of them in existence.

Do people tend to recognise you in the street, and is it embarrassing?

Yes, they do recognise me—and no, it isn't embarrassing. Why should it be? It's a really nice thing to happen.

Which of your records do you like best?

'Get It On', I suppose—I still like that one. But I always like the record that's most recently made, which is 'Telegram Sam' at the moment.

How do you think pop music will develop?

It's impossible to predict fashions in music. But musicians are freeing themselves more and more from the 'business' side of making records. That's really the key—the musician will get more freedom to do what interests him, rather than what the businessman thinks will be successful.

If you could live your life again, would you change anything?

Maybe I'd make a few business changes, but personally I'm enjoying it as it is—no changes.

The Marc Bolan Story

PAUL McCARTNEY is said to have called Tyrannosaurus Rex (T. Rex as they are now known) 'the new generation's Beatles'. Marc Bolan, the backbone of the group has been called 'a curly headed waif,' 'a little elf,' 'a wizard,' and even 'the elfin prince'.

Partly all this fairy-tale talk is due to Marc's size. He's only five feet tall. But there's a lot more to it than that. Marc has always been interested in stories of magic and has written poetry and songs that tell of strange people, creatures and countries. Even his early record titles show it. His first record, made in 1965, was called 'The Wizard'. Then there was 'My People Were Fair, And Had Sky in Their Hair, But Now They're Content to Wear Stars on Their Brows'—and that's just the title! Next came 'Prophets, Seers and Sages, the Angels of the Ages'. Then, simply 'Unicorn'.

Marc Bolan was born in Stoke Newington, London — though his real name at that time was Marc Feld. When he was nine, he would visit a famous pop-stars' coffee bar in London to see 'all my heroes'. He was even allowed to work there, pouring out the coffees and listening to the music. Playing there was a young singer called Harry Webb who later changed his name to Cliff Richard.

"I only used to go and work there for the music—and the juke box, which in those days was dynamite!"

All this star-gazing came to an end when he was moved to a new school in Wimbledon. He happily confesses that he hated it. His frequent absences turned into a permanent state, and Marc decided to become a child model. At thirteen he was introduced to the public as 'the face of the new youth'—and earned quite a lot of money at it.

He even did a little acting in those days—though in non-speaking parts. But underneath it all, his real passion was to make records. His mother had bought him a guitar but he had not taken much notice of it at first.

"I got the name 'Tyrannosaurus Rex' out of a book. When I was eleven I had measles and I had to stay in bed, and I told my mother to get me a dinosaur book from the library." There he found a picture of a Tyrannosaurus Rex and underneath read 'this is the biggest creature that ever walked the earth.' Marc stored that name in the back of his head.

Top pop-star of 1971, Marc and his group first hit the jackpot with 'Ride a White Swan', then 'Hot Love' and 'Get it On', and 'Jeepster'.

Marc has already had published one book of poems and is working on another. He wears his long hair in dripping, unkempt curls. "I never bother to comb it," he says. In fact hairdressers all over the country are doing a roaring trade in Bolan-style wigs, it seems. The other fashion trend that some of Marc's more adventurous followers have taken up is the use of glitter in their make-up. He wears sequins on his cheeks, perched like teardrops.

The T. Rex fan club address is now at Suite B, 7 Charles Street, London W.1.

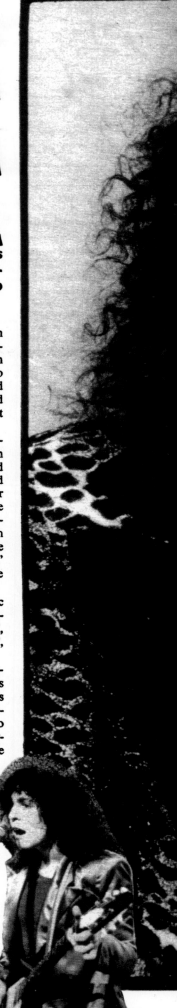

With Marc in the above picture is Micky Finn.

□□□□□□□□□□□□□□□□□□□□□□□□□□□□□□□□□□

Toys and Games Competition

Just a reminder to send in entries to the Magpie Toys and Games Competition by the 24th February. A sketch and short description of the toy or game which you have invented should be sent to:— Magpie Toys and Games Competition, Thames Television, Teddington Lock, Middlesex.

And don't forget that if the winning game or toy is good enough, it will be put into general production by a leading manufacturer.

□□□□□□□□□□□□□□□□□□□□□□□□□□□□□□□□□□

Magpie Appeal

£28,382—that is the amazing sum which Magpie viewers have sent in for this year's Appeal on behalf of deaf children. When the Appeal was launched on 30th November an initial target of £1,280 was set up. This was the sum needed to buy twenty machines which would help teachers in special schools for the deaf up and down the country to teach the children how to talk. As you read in LOOK-IN deaf children do not know what speech sounds like and so cannot talk, without special tuition.

One week, after the Appeal was launched, almost twice the amount of the original target was reached. Magpie viewers rallied round and raised money by every sort of activity imaginable.

By the time the Appeal closed on January 11, scores of valuable machines had been bought and dis-patched. The teachers at the special schools were deeply grateful. But above all, it is the children themselves whom your efforts have helped. Their future will be a little easier thanks to all of you who contributed.

23rd September 1972 • Art: Arthur Ranson • Story: Geoff Cowan

High-speed humour with some motorway madness next week !

PARDON MY GENIE

*H*OW *would you like to have a genie at your command—a powerful sorcerer, able to make your every wish come true? You think it would be marvellous? Then you can't have been watching Thames Television's hilarious series* Pardon My Genie *over the last few weeks.*

The trouble with the genie that young Hal Adden discovered when he tried to polish the old watering can in Mister Cobbledick's shop is that he's four thousand years old—and his magic, like the watering can, is a bit rusty. Not only that: he's inclined to take everything Hal says at face value. You know how often we say things we don't really mean, exclamations like 'Strike Me Pink!' or 'Stone Me!' Well, say that kind of thing when you have a genie under your control, and you're likely to find yourself the colour of a raspberry yoghurt and being bombarded with boulders! ➤➤➤➤

Roy Barraclough plays the unfortunate Mr. Cobbledick (right).

20th May 1972

PARDON MY GENIE

←◀◀◀ If we can believe the genie's story, he was once the slave of the magic lamp owned by Aladdin, Prince of China. Over the centuries, the metal of the lamp has been used to make all sorts of things—including a plough, a drainpipe and a back door key—but the genie has remained bound to serve the owner of whatever object is made from the magical metal.

Genie or Jinee

What *is* a genie, anyway? Well, in Arabic legend there were powerful spirits, some good and some evil, who lived in the mountains of Kâf, at the edge of the earth. (When the legends were first told, most people believed that the earth was flat, and that there were mountains around the edge to stop unwary travellers from falling off!) These spirits were called *jinn*, the singular of which is *jinee*, or 'genie'.

You'll find lots of stories about *jinn* in the collection of Eastern legends called *The Arabian Nights Entertainments* or *The Thousand and One Nights*. These stories, which include such familiar tales as those of 'Aladdin', 'Sinbad the Sailor' and 'Ali Baba and the Forty Thieves', were first written down in Egypt, about six hundred years ago. They are supposed to have been told by the beautiful princess Scheherazade to the cruel Sultan Schahriah, who had condemned her to death. But Scheherazade told such exciting stories every night, that the Sultan kept putting off the execution in order to hear more.

You've probably seen the pantomime version of 'Aladdin', in which he is the son of a poor Chinese washerwoman, the comical Widow Twankey. In the *Arabian Nights*, he is an Arabic boy who, because of the riches he gains through the magic lamp, is able to marry the daughter of the Sultan of China.

Long-lost lamp

The idea of Aladdin's lamp turning up centuries later in England was used by the famous Victorian writer, F. E. Anstey, in his book *The Brass Bottle*. He tells how the genie was let out in 19th-century London by a young architect, whose life was made a misery by the genie's blundering attempts to reward him. Although *The Brass Bottle* was written about eighty years ago, it's still as funny as ever; your local library will probably have a copy.

Now, in *Pardon My Genie*, writer Bob Block has brought us up to date on the wanderings of Aladdin's faithful servant. Hugh Paddick, who plays the well-meaning genie, is one of the fine all-rounders of British acting. His successes range from leading rôles in revue and musical comedy—he spent over three years as 'Colonel Pickering' in the London stage production of *My Fair Lady* — to important parts in Shakesperian productions, television and movies. He revealed himself as a man of many voices, all of them funny, in such radio series as *Stop Messing About*.

Hal Adden ('Al-Addin, get it?) is played by twenty-eight-year-old Ellis Jones, his first leading rôle on television. Both Ellis and Roy Barraclough (Mister Cobbledick) came up the hard way in the acting profession, with long years of solid work in provincial repertory theatres.

Hal Adden (Ellis Jones) introduces the genie to modern 'magic'.

Will the genie get his sorcery straightened out in time to help Hal win the hand of the lovely Patricia Cobbledick? Or will this magical misfit and cock-eyed conjurer drive Hal and Mister Cobbledick—who is so often the victim of his mistakes—up the wall first? Keep watching—and you may find out.

FROM THE HORSE'S MOUTH

This week, we look at Dora's horse — Copper

There they were, these people from a television company, taking me away from Mount Pleasant Stud as cool as you please! Hang it, I was quite happy there. I didn't want to be moved. So I played up a bit. Copper Prince is my name, and I thought I'd jolly well teach them all to bow down in front of 'royalty'. I could sense it, you know. They were *frightened* of me! So when they climbed on my back, I jumped about and made myself a devil of a nuisance—until this girl Gillian Blake (she's called Dora in the series) came up. She was very gentle and quiet, and I knew right away that I could make her my friend. Now Gillian's got me for her very own, and eventually, she's going to take me down to Guildford, in Surrey. She lives in London, but she says the big city's no place for a horse. I couldn't agree with her more. I'd have a *right* old job finding water buckets to hoof around in Piccadilly Circus!

THE ADVENTURES of Black Beauty

A search of the grounds is made!

A STRANGE NEWCOMER TO THE FIVE OAK'S AREA, MR. KILNER, CHAINS HIS GATES, FENCES HIS PROPERTY WITH BARBED WIRE, AND REFUSES TO ADMIT CALLERS! JENNY AND KEVIN GORDON, AND THEIR FRIENDS, NED AND ALBERT, ARE INTRIGUED... AND PREDICTABLY, THEY FORM THEIR OWN WILD CONCLUSIONS...

EITHER HE'S A MASTER CRIMINAL...

A FOREIGN SPY MAKING BOMBS...

A FORGER...

OR HE'S GOT SOMEONE THERE HELD PRISONER!

REMEMBER—WHEN WE CALLED, HE SAID: "WE DON'T WANT ANY VISITORS." SO NOW WE'VE AGREED WE'LL TAKE A CLOSER LOOK...

TONIGHT! THERE MAY BE NO TIME TO LOSE! LET'S WORK OUT A DETAILED PLAN...

WHEN THE SUN HAS GONE DOWN AND THE COUNTRYSIDE IS QUIET...

THERE'S THE FENCE! TIME YOU DID YOUR STUFF, JENNY!

COME ON, BEAUTY. IT WON'T BE THE FIRST TIME YOU'VE JUMPED IN THE DARK!

THIS IS A GREAT IDEA! IF WE'RE CAUGHT SNOOPING AROUND KILNER'S GROUNDS, WE SAY WE'RE AFTER BEAUTY...

...WHO GOT OUT OF HIS PADDOCK AND JUMPED THIS FENCE WHILE WE WERE CHASING HIM! A PERFECT ALIBI!

NEXT MOMENT...

NOW, BEAUTY... HUPP!

ON THE FAR SIDE, JENNY SLIDES OFF BEAUTY'S BACK...

YOU'RE TO STAY HERE! UNDERSTAND? JUST WAIT FOR US, AND WE'LL BE BACK AS SOON AS WE CAN!

HNFFFF HNEEEE

12th October 1974 • Art: Mike Noble • Story: Angus P. Allan

More Black Beauty thrills on page 40

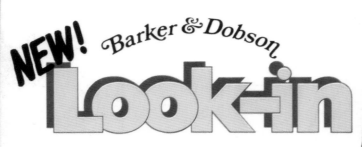

JUNIOR CINEMA

Twinkle, Twinkle, Little Star . . .!

☆ If you listen to enough disc-jockey shows on the radio, sooner or later you'll probably hear a tinkly tune, sung in a giggly little girl's voice, called 'On the Good Ship Lollipop'. But the chances are that this simple, attractive little ditty is being played for a listener old enough to be your grandad — for it was recorded nearly forty years ago by a wonder girl called Shirley Temple.

When six-year-old Shirley hit the movie screens in the mid-1930s, the 'child star' was something new. But grown-up screen stars soon found to their cost that a kid with a cheeky smile could be guaranteed to steal a scene from the most accomplished actor — and win the hearts of audiences all over the world.

This week, Granada Television's *Clapperboard* series looks at the great child stars, from curly-topped Shirley to a present-day favourite, Jack Wild. Jack will be in the studio to talk about his film career, and you can see clips from OLIVER, FLIGHT OF THE DOVES and Jack's very first film, DANNY THE DRAGON.

Shirley Temple, as HEIDI: a super-star aged six.

Saturday Morning Special

If you are among the more than 400,000 children who go to the special Saturday morning shows that many cinemas run for young audiences, then you may have seen Jack Wild's screen début. For DANNY THE DRAGON was made by the Children's Film Foundation as a ten-part serial for Saturday morning audiences.

Special film shows for children were pioneered by Granada Cinemas as long ago as 1927. Later, J. Arthur Rank set up a special department within the Rank Organisation to make films for children. Then, in 1951, all branches of the British film industry agreed to finance the Children's Film Foundation (CFF).

To date, the CFF has produced nearly one hundred feature films, thirty serials and many 'shorts'. Among the CCF's discoveries—like Jack Wild—are Francesca Annis, Michael Crawford, Susan George, Olivia Hussey and Carol White.

In DANNY THE DRAGON, his first film, Jack Wild befriends a visitor from outer space.

The Movie-Makers—II: The First 'Cinema'

☆☆☆☆☆☆☆☆☆☆☆☆

Having invented a movie camera, William Kennedy Dixon set to work on a 'projector', so that pictures could be thrown upon a screen and viewed by more than one person at a time. He came up with what he called the 'kinetoscope'.

By 1894, the first 'kinetoscope parlour', ancestor of the modern cinema, had opened in New York. Dixon set up the first American film studio —the Black Maria Studio, New Jersey—to supply it with films. His early films, showing famous entertainers of the time like Buffalo Bill and sharp-shooting Annie Oakley, only lasted for about fifteen *seconds* each.

Meanwhile, inventors in other countries had been working along the same lines. In France, the Lumière brothers improved on Dixon's process by reducing the number of 'frames' that needed to pass through the projector every second. This made it possible to show longer movies while still only using the same 'footage', or length of film.

Invisible Man

Coming shortly—a new laughter-raiser from Walt Disney.

Due for release in a few weeks is NOW YOU SEE HIM, NOW YOU DON'T. As the title suggests, the theme is a variation on the 'invisible man' story.

Kurt Russell—recently seen in THE COMPUTER WORE TENNIS SHOES—stars as the student. Among the supporting actors is Cesar Romero, whom you may remember as that master-criminal 'The Joker' in the *Batman* television series.

Not an accident victim (left) – but a 'visible' invisible man!

On the Small Screen

Here are some of the feature films you can see on television this week. (Please note all details correct at time of going to press.)
Friday, May 19
7.30 p.m. (Wales/West)
PORT AFRIQUE.
Sunday, May 21
2.55 p.m. (Granada)
SECRET PEOPLE
3.00 p.m. (Scottish)
LITTLE BIG SHOT
3.15 p.m. (Midland)
VILLAGE OF DAUGHTERS
3.15 p.m. (Wales/West)
THE HONEYMOON MACHINE (with Steve McQueen).
3.15 p.m. (Border)
HALF ANGEL
7.55 p.m. (Midland)
THE DOUBLE MAN
7.55 p.m. (Granada)
MY GEISHA
7.55 p.m. (Wales/West)
VICKI (a 'who-dunnit').
7.55 p.m. (Border)
A PRIZE OF ARMS
Tuesday, May 23
6.20 p.m. (Scottish)
CHARGE OF THE LANCERS
7.00 p.m. (Border)
BLUEPRINT FOR ROBBERY
7.00 p.m. (Granada)
GREEN HELL
7.05 p.m. (Wales/West)
YUMA (with Clint Walker).
Thursday, May 25
7.00 p.m. (Scottish)
ONE-MAN MUTINY
7.05 p.m. (Wales/West)
STRATEGIC AIR COMMAND
7.15 p.m. (Border)
A TOUCH OF LARCENY
7.30 p.m. (Midland)
TIMETABLE (thriller).

What will the potion do to Nicholas? See page 48

Man About the House

Paula Wilcox
Richard O'Sullivan
Sally Thomsett

For all Follyfoot fans

'Follyfoot' has temporarily left your television screens, but LOOK-IN will be continuing the strip cartoon adventures of this very popular series. Judging by the many requests in our postbag each week, it would seem that most LOOK-IN readers would like to know more about the three stars of 'Follyfoot'.
Here then are a few facts about Gillian Blake, Steve Hodson and Christian Rodska.

GILLIAN (DORA)

★An only child, Gillian Blake was born in Buckingham and started riding when she was five. She attended a two year course at the Guildhall School of Music and Drama, and took time off during her last term to appear in a TV play. This role put her in the running for 'Follyfoot', which required her to 'take up the reins' all over again, as she hadn't ridden for several years. Gillian has made numerous TV appearances, not to mention the film 'Goodbye Mr. Chips', which starred Peter O'Toole. Currently living in London, she shares her home with 'Shella', an Afghan Hound, and her two Siamese cats, 'Bengo' and 'Jasmin'. Her ambition is simply 'to keep working', but when she isn't doing that she likes to read or go horse-riding. Gillian also uses her chocolate-brown Mini 1000 for getting about, though she 'can't stand traffic jams'. The car's colour serves as a reminder of her liking for chocolates!

On the fashion front, Gillian usually wears jeans and a T-shirt or jumper, but when it comes to dresses she 'prefers longer things'.

CHRISTIAN (RON)

★Christian Rodska hails from Newcastle-on-Tyne. He attended school both in this country and abroad, for his Danish-born father was once captain of the Royal Yacht of King Feisal of Iraq, and his seafaring role has led the Rodskas to travel all over the world. Having a wide experience in repertory, Christian first appeared on TV in a play called 'A Beast With Two Backs'. Later small-screen credits include parts in such series as 'Z Cars' and 'Hadleigh'. His 'mount' in 'Follyfoot' is not so much of the four-legged variety but a motor-bike which he proudly rebuilt after buying it for £5. Christian also fences, swims, skis and skates, enjoys archery and, for less vigorous entertainment, paints.

STEVE

★It was chance which first led Bradford-born Steve Hodson to learn to ride, a 'qualification' which certainly helped him secure his role in 'Follyfoot'. While waiting to start work at drama school, Steve stayed with a family in Wimbledon who happened to have a stable in their extensive garden. So Steve used to saddle up, 'to pass the time'. His first minor involvement in amateur dramatics was a bit of backstage work in a production of 'Faustus' by the Belle Vue Grammar School. Then he joined a theatre workshop at the Bradford Civic Playhouse. A growing interest inspired Steve to eventually study at the Central School of Speech and Drama in London, where he played a vast range of characters. His TV appearances include a walk-on part in the 'Hine' series and a more substantial role in a play called 'The Grievance'. Off-stage, Steve has turned his hand to working as a scaffolder, navvy and butcher, though he relaxes by reading, writing poetry and, of course, horse-riding.

YOUR VIEW

This week, Judi Bowker, 'Vicky' in London Weekend Television's 'Black Beauty' series, makes the selection of letters, jokes and pictures from the LOOK-IN Postbag—including the £2 Star Letter...

"I bet it's a baby giraffe."
**Anita Liversidge,
Barnsley, Yorks.**

STAR LETTER

My mum had an old bowl which she thought might be valuable. She took it to an antique shop, where the lady in charge said that it was hardly more than 'a cracked piece of kitchenware'. She offered fifteen shillings (this was just before 'new pence' appeared) for it, and mum accepted. Some weeks later, mum went back to the same shop intending to buy a present for someone. The same lady in charge produced the very same bowl that mum had sold her (except that a crack had been carefully painted over)—and asked nine pounds for it!

**William S. Richardson,
Wilberton, Yorkshire.**

★ Not necessarily 'antique' but certainly an *old* trick, William. Still, at least you've won the £2 star prize!

OLD TIMER

I look after an old horse, of which I am the part owner. He is forty years old, but still going strong, and his name is 'Dandy'. He lives alone in a field, but he has lots of company because about fourteen horses belonging to a riding stable live on the other side of the fence. He's very happy, and I'm sure he'll live to a ripe old age.

**Tina Carter,
High Wycombe,
Buckinghamshire.**

★ I'd say he was doing pretty well already, Tina—but I wish him lots more happy years. And thank you for sending us the picture of yourself with Dandy and Sophie, your dog.

BLACKOUT

I have come to a conclusion that there is a 'jinx' on our television set, because during the last three episodes of 'Follyfoot' — my favourite programme — the set has 'packed up' halfway through. So far, I've managed to retrieve the situation by dashing down the road to watch the rest of the programme at my aunt's house—but what's going to happen next week, when my aunt goes on holiday?

**'Anonymous',
Stirchley, Birmingham.**

★ Well, Anonymous, at least the goblin that haunts your TV has now earned you £1—but you'll need to send your name to the editor so that he can forward your prize.

"I don't like the colour!"
**Tony Arber,
Huddersfield, Yorkshire.**

RECORD SPOT

My mum and dad still have some of the old 78 rpm records, including Elvis Presley's 'Heartbreak Hotel', Buddy Holly's 'It Really Doesn't Matter Any More' and the Everley Brothers' 'Bye Bye Love'. Isn't it strange how old tunes keep coming back into fashion.

**Carol Ingram,
Ringmer, Sussex.**

★ Sounds like your mum and dad are 'rock 'n' roll' fans, Carol —and the editor tells me that all 'rock 'n' rollers' are in for a treat in LOOK-IN in a few weeks' time!

CHEWED UP

Our class at school keeps gerbils. One day, someone poked the corner of the classroom curtain into the cage and the next day our teacher found that the gerbils had chewed an enormous hole in it. We had to mend the hole in our needlework lesson.

**Mandy Benham,
Chinnor, Oxfordshire.**

★ Just in case any LOOK-IN readers don't know what a gerbil looks like, here is a picture of one.

THAT ACE OF WANDS MAGIC

Master magician 'Tarot' (Michael Mackenzie, right) is joined by newcomers to this series, 'Chas'—actor Roy Holder (top, left) —and 'Mikki', played by Petra Markham.

THINK ABOUT A VERY BUSY MARKET-PLACE. What's the first thing that comes to mind? The bright awnings over the stalls and the kaleidoscope of colours on barrows selling flowers and fruit? Or is it, perhaps, the noise, with boxes and crates clattering on the pavement and stall-holders yelling the praises of their wares? Or maybe you think first of the dense crowds of people milling around, looking for a bargain?

But now, think about the same market at night, when everyone has gone home and the stalls are bare. The lightest footfall echoes through the empty market-place and strange shadows dance across the littered ground. It could be pretty spooky, alone there in the dark.

Watney Street Market, off the Commercial Road in the London district of Wapping, is the setting for Thames Television's new *Ace Of Wands* series, beginning next Wednesday in all regions. For the purposes of the story, it's certainly a sinister place, supposed to be haunted by ➤➤➤

the ghost of a long-dead miser, a restless, evil spirit whose nightly wanderings turn fresh food rotten overnight and send ornaments and crockery crashing to the floor.

As before, 'Tarot' the master magician is played by Michael MacKenzie, whom you may remember reading about in LOOK-IN, last July. But 'Lulli' and 'Sam', his assistants in the previous series, have left him. 'Lulli', we learn, is now married, and 'Sam' has gone into road haulage.

There's danger in plenty, to both mind and body, in the sinister market, so Tarot soon enlists the aid of two young helpers, 'Mikki' (played by Petra Markham) and 'Chas' (played by Roy Holder), a brother and sister who live in the market and are anxious to save it from possible demolition.

" 'Mikki'," says Petra Markham, whom you may remember as 'Lydia', the youngest daughter of a Victorian family in the comedy series ALBERT AND VICTORIA, "is a bit scatty. She's romantic and dreamy—a bit like me." 'Mikki' is also

Chas, played by Roy Holder, is exposed to danger.

psychic: sometimes she gets a brief glimpse of the future.

"I don't really know whether I believe in the supernatural or not," says Petra. "I've had one or two dreams which seem to have foretold coming events—and last year I had my fortune told with Tarot cards (the ancient fortune-telling picture cards from which 'Tarot' takes his name), which turned up several correct prophecies."

Supernatural Story

Roy Holder, who plays 'Chas', is more definite. "I think there must be something in the supernatural. After all, thousands of strange happenings are reported—and only one needs to be true to show that it's not all a load of rubbish. Like many actors, I'm very superstitious. When I was filming in Singapore and India, I had my palm read by Eastern fortune-tellers, but I'm afraid I only listened to the *good* things they told me."

But Roy has an even stronger reason for believing that there may be some truth in 'magic'. "One of my neighbours, an old lady, often visits a gypsy fortune-teller. Some time ago, she warned me that the fortune-teller had told her that a local house would be burgled and that 'the dogs would not bark'.

"A few weeks later, I was invited to a party given by the landlord of a local pub. While we were all having a good time downstairs, thieves broke into the rooms above and stole £250. And the landlord's two ferocious alsatians, kept specially as guard dogs, didn't utter so much as a yelp!"

And that just goes to show, there might be more to the mystery and magic of 'Ace of Wands' than meets the eye.

From the first series of 'Follyfoot'—and for this water-bound sequence an 'extra' horse is used.

The Colonel's horse (right) tolerates being led by Slugger, while 'Dino', held by Ron Stryker, seems more interested in the conversation with Dora.

...ide of Follyfoot...

FROM THE HORSE'S MOUTH

'Brown Forrester' enjoys the Colonel riding him—but it's a different story if anyone else tries to mount up!

This week completes the series with
the rest of us!

HULLO, THERE! This is Folly, *and I'm not a year old yet. I'm only a foal, but since I've more or less the same name as the series, I'm going to do the talking.*

Actually, nobody dares to stop me—because I've quite a temper, and at the slightest opportunity, I kick things.

I've kicked most of the other horses in my time, and I'm not afraid of anything. I've even kicked the old mangle standing in the yard. You ask Slugger (*he* calls me names I'd rather not repeat).

Of course, I'm not the only Follyfoot horse who acts up a bit. Take Ron Stryker's chestnut for example. She's called *Socks*. I well remember the day Steve was riding her, and he thought he'd take her over an easy fence. Well, *Socks* didn't fancy that at all, so she stopped short and hurled him—just a week after throwing Dora, too!

Good job, I say! We horses occasionally like to make it quite clear who's boss around here!

Actually, I shouldn't be so mischievous. We're looked after very well, and the people are really nice to us. We have lovely stables with all mod cons, and plenty of fodder and grooming. The actors are very considerate to us, on the whole. For example, they know we're inclined to be nervous when cameras and things come poking from all directions. You should have seen Steve making sure that his own horse, *Alex*, didn't get nervous. He spent hours with Alex out in a field, getting him used to microphone booms by waving a branch about over his head. By the time filming started, *Alex* was as calm as anything!

They take account of our feelings, too. For instance, when one of the television stories made it necessary for a horse called *Kip* to swim through a river, *Kip* didn't really fancy a bath—so in the end, they altered the shooting to close-ups, and let him stay on dry land while people squirted water around to make it look as though he was in the stream.

You've already met *Alex* and *Copper Prince*—that's Dora's horse. There's also *Brown Forrester*. He's the one the Colonel rides. Won't let anyone else up in the saddle, but he'll tolerate Slugger as long as he's just being led. Then there are our two donkeys, *Bubble* and *Squeak*, but they keep very much to themselves.

We're all looked after by a girl called Jane Royston, who's the Horse Manager for Folly-

Horse Manager, Jane Royston

foot. She lives here during the making of the series—as we all do. Whenever Follyfoot's not being filmed, we go off to livery stables, but I suppose Jane has a human-type home to live in!

Oh! I nearly forgot! There's one horse here who even had *me* beaten for naughtiness once. That's *Sultan*, the grey. Well, we were filming a scene, and the people wanted him to move across camera. But he wouldn't. So the Colonel popped up and gave him a sly pinch on the hindquarters in the hope that it would make him go. All *Sultan* did was turn round and use his teeth to pinch the Colonel right back! Everyone laughed—including Steve—and it must have irritated old *Sultan*, 'cos he stepped forward and gave Steve a nip for good measure. Nobody told him off, of course—because he'd walked neatly across camera to do it—just like they wanted! It's a jolly good life, being an actor-horse!

Is Beauty going for help? See page 52

26th October 1974

Gang-Up with the Groups!

Slade, T Rex, The Faces, the Jackson Five, to mention but a few, stand out as the BIG star names of the pop world. But many other groups are making their presence felt in the charts . . . groups that are rapidly becoming everyone's favourites.

STATUS QUO

Believe it or not, Status Quo have been together as a band for nearly ten years and have now reached an established position as a leading live and recording group. In all that time, only one change has been made in the line-up.

The group's music has a rough, powerhouse drive to it and as the press handouts say: 'They go straight in for the attack, know how to make a musical killing and give their audiences something stimulating to watch and something tough to boogie to.'

FOCUS

Focus, the Dutch quartet with the sound that is so startlingly different it's been described as 'a powerful driving instrumental sound lightened by brilliant phonetic vocal effects'—is here to stay. Focus began life in 1969 as backing band for the Dutch version of the stage musical 'Hair'.

When the four musicians left the show to concentrate on their own style, their impact in Britain was slow at first but hard work, two exhausting British club dates and records that sold consistently well over many months paid off for them last year, when they scooped the award for the Brightest Hope of 1972 in the *Melody Maker* Poll. Earlier that year at the Reading Jazz Festival they stopped the show and made every other act—some exalted names among them— realize their true potential.

Thijs Van Leer, the group's founder, is a former member of the Dutch Conservatorium of Music, and writes a great deal of Focus material. Jan Akkerman (lead guitar) and Pierre Van Der Linden (drums) were both formerly in another Dutch band called Brainbox, while Burt Reiter came on the scene last year, replacing Cyril Havermans.

1973 began in a big way for the group—with their first British concert tour, taking in 21 concerts in 23 dates. Their latest release 'Sylvia' is having its impact on the charts and indeed at one stage recently Focus were the first group since the Shadows to have two instrumental hits at the same time.

Above, left, in the studio with Focus. Left to right are Pierre Van Der Linden, Burt Reiter, Jan Akkerman, Thijs Van Leer. Left, Status Quo consisting of Rick Parfitt, Alan Lancaster, John Goghlan and Mike Rossi.

BLACKFOOT SUE

The great 'Sue' uprising began when a four-piece band from Birmingham—home of groups like The Moody Blues, Black Sabbath and the Move—changed its name from Gift to Blackfoot Sue. They also began working under a new producer and a new record label (JAM). Their first single was a composition of their own called 'Standing In The Road', which, despite the usual setbacks confronting an unknown group with a first record, pushed its way into the top ten.

The boys—Dave Farmer, drums; brother Tom, bass guitar; Eddie Golga, lead guitar, and Alan Jones, rhythm guitar—have just finished work on their first album.

Blackfoot Sue right—(left to right) Dave Farmer, Alan Jones, Eddie Golga and Tom Farmer.

Roy Wood

WIZZARD

In June of last year, with ELO an actuality and a much praised working unit, Roy Wood handed over leadership of the band to Jeff Lynne, and went on to form Wizzard. And it certainly is a suitable name for the combination of hard rock and experiments which resulted! The group's first single on the Harvest label 'Ball Park Incident', was warmly received by the fans and the LP 'Wizzard's Brew' cemented Wizzard as a force in the pop world. Wizzard consists of Roy Wood, vocals, guitar; Rick Price, vocals, bass; Bill Hunt, piano; Hugh McDowell, electric cello; Mike Bernie, tenor, alto and baritone saxes; Nick Pentelow, tenor sax; Keith Smart, drums, and Charlie Grima, drums.

ROXY MUSIC

Roxy Music originated in the winter of 1970-71, with clear cut aims in mind —" a fusion of older rock 'n' roll idioms with a powerful battery of electronic and synthesised sound ". The group's first LP 'Roxy Music' was released by Island Records in June of last year.

Latest single is 'Pyjamarama', written by Bryan Ferry—and 'For Your Pleasure' is Roxy's newest album. The group made its official debut, by the way, on the main stage at the Great Western Express Festival in Lincolnshire on May 27.

Roxy Music—(back row, left to right) Phil Manzenera, Bryan Ferry, Paul Thompson, (front row) Eno and Andy Mackay.

14th April 1973

51

Meeting The Saturday Scene Stars

AN EXCLUSIVE LOOK-IN RECORD PREVIEW

WHAT HAVE ALVIN STARDUST, Gary Glitter, David Cassidy, Sweet, Sparks and Showaddywaddy in common? Apart from being very successful hitmakers, that is! The answer is that they are all interviewed by Sally James on a great new LP "Saturday Scene" which should be in your local record shop at the beginning of November.

A few weeks ago, when Sally interviewed Alvin Stardust and Ron and Russell Mael of Sparks for the album, Look-in was invited along to Sarm recording studios to join in the fun and take some pictures. Alvin chatted about his former career (he was once known as Shane Fenton, remember) and just how he chose the name Alvin Stardust. Ron and Russell, as is usual whenever we see them, were talking about food. Russell, in fact, spends a lot of his spare time preparing various dishes, mainly sweet ones, while Ron likes to occupy himself sampling his brother's creations. Young Cooks among you will be interested to note that Russell gives one of his recipes, 'Creme Caramel' for 45 people—just the thing for breaking the ice at parties—on the "Saturday Scene" album.

⫸⫸⫸

⫸ ⟶ Sweet thoughts bring Brian Connolly and friends to mind. Brian, Mick, Steve and Andy all talk to Sally about themselves, as do Showaddywaddy — you wouldn't think you could get that many people on one record, would you? Like Alvin, Showaddywaddy explain how they chose their name, and tell us what they think of the States. "We all live in estates!"

David Cassidy, in an exclusive interview, talks about touring, animals and his fans, while Garry Glitter tells us how he likes to relax — among other things.

We thought that it was a terrific idea to put interviews of your favourite stars all on one record — and certainly at £1.99 it would make a great Christmas present to give or receive — so we talked to Saturday Scene producer Warren Breach about how the record idea came about.

"Sally's live interviews have become, perhaps, the most popular part of "Saturday Scene". It's nice, after all, to be able to see what pop stars are really like — you might see and hear them at gigs and concerts, as well as performing their latest number on TV, but you never get to know them that way."

"I thought that, in view of the many requests from viewers to have their favourite stars appear again, it

David Cassidy

would be a good idea to put some interviews on a record, so that you can listen to them as often as you like. I always look on 'Saturday Scene' as belonging to our viewers and, as far as possible, try to give them what they want. Unfortunately, 'Saturday Scene' is for London viewers only, but the 'Saturday Scene' album isn't, so I'd be delighted to hear what Look-in readers think of it, as well as suggestions as to who else they would like to hear interviewed. Perhaps then, this could be the first of a series of 'Saturday Scene' LPs.

"Look-in have given us a lot of valuable help with this album, and you can help even more by sending me your comments."

(Letters should be addressed to Warren Breach, c/o LOOK-IN, 247 Tottenham Court Road, London W1P 0AU.)

The album also features a couple of songs by Sally James and two more by a great new group Love Together.

Sally sings "Isn't It Good" and "Wake Me When It's Over", both of which will also be released on a single, as will Love Together's two numbers "Round Ev'ry Corner" and "Blackjack". Love Together are the two girls and three boys featured in this week's colour pin-up.

Showaddywaddy

Sally with album producer Mike Smith and recording engineer Gary Lyons.

The Sweet

Gary Glitter

LOVE TOGETHER are, from left to right: Jess Richer, Nichola Martin, Steve Glen, Liz Robertson and Dave Reece. Their first record "Round Ev'ry Corner" is the theme music for London Weekend Television's new series London Bridge.

The Adventures of Black Beauty

BELIEVING HIM TO BE HOLDING A SMALL BOY PRISONER, JENNY AND KEVIN 'INVESTIGATE' THE MYSTERIOUS MR. KILNER. FALLING FOUL OF HIS WITCH-LIKE COMPANION, THE SINISTER MOTHER DENCH, THEY ARE LOCKED IN A CELLAR. THEN, TO THEIR SURPRISE, THEY DISCOVER THAT KILNER SEEMS JUST AS SCARED OF THE OLD WOMAN AS *THEY* ARE!

MY SON NICHOLAS LIES UPSTAIRS — WASTING FROM THE DISEASE THAT KILLED HIS MOTHER AND SISTER IN LONDON! MY ONLY HOPE IS MOTHER DENCH'S POWERS!

BUT- BUT WHAT DOES SHE KNOW ABOUT MEDICINE..?

SHE KNOWS THE OLD WAYS... THE FORGOTTEN SKILLS OF THE ANCIENTS! I'M CONVINCED...

IF SHE'S SO GOOD, WHY'S SHE KEEPING US PRISONER?

MR. KILNER... ARE YOU PAYING MOTHER DENCH AN AWFUL LOT OF MONEY FOR HER SERVICES?...

MEANWHILE, UPSTAIRS IN NICHOLAS'S BEDROOM...

HEE HEE HEE! WHEN I TELL HIM I MUST GO TO A SECRET PLACE AND BUY COSTLY INGREDIENTS, HE WILL PART UP WITH THE REST OF HIS MONEY... WILLINGLY! AND THEN I SHALL JUST DISAPPEAR...

DRINK, MY BOY! IT WILL MAKE YOU WORSE... MUCH WORSE! AND THEN I SHALL BE ABLE TO TWIST YOUR FATHER ROUND MY LITTLE FINGER!

AS THE EVIL OLD WOMAN BEGINS HER PLOY TO SWINDLE KILNER OUT OF THE LAST OF HIS SAVINGS, THERE COMES A KNOCK AT THE DOOR!

PERHAPS THE BRAT WILL RECOVER OF HIS OWN ACCORD... PERHAPS NOT! IT IS OF NO INTEREST TO MOTHER DENCH!

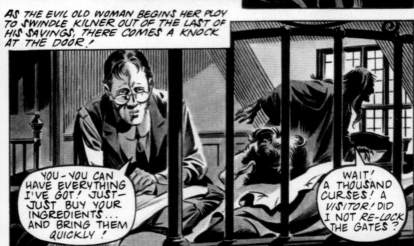

YOU- YOU CAN HAVE EVERYTHING I'VE GOT! JUST- JUST BUY YOUR INGREDIENTS... AND BRING THEM QUICKLY!

WAIT! A THOUSAND CURSES! A VISITOR! DID I NOT RE-LOCK THE GATES?

Another exciting adventure next week!

Sally with Brian Connolly and Andy Scott of Sweet.

Wimbledon's very own Wombles!

The Saturday Scene Roadshow

IT'S ALL HAPPENING FOR WIMBLEDON, isn't it? First the Wombles, then a football team that so nearly beat mighty Leeds United in those memorable cup-ties, and now the "Saturday Scene Roadshow".

The first couple of "Roadshows" at the Wimbledon Theatre have proved so popular that they will be held regularly during the next few months — and with surprise star guests like the Rollers and Sweet appearing in the first of these great Saturday spectaculars, it's no wonder!

The "Roadshow" is based on London Weekend Television's "Saturday Scene", and is presented by Sally James, with help from David Bridger of Bell Records. The "Roadshows" start at 2.30 on Saturday afternoons, and always promise exciting surprise star guests. The names of the guests will always be a closely guarded secret, but each "Roadshow" will have a live group, records, a pop quiz, a dance competition, and lots of fantastic prizes. Oh, and by the way, those furry Wimbledon Wombles will be there, too!

Details of the "Saturday Scene Roadshow" and how to obtain tickets will be given regularly on "Saturday Scene", and you can also buy tickets at the Box Office, Wimbledon Theatre, The Broadway, Wimbledon, SW19. Price 75p.

Many Look-in readers will not get the chance to see one of the "Roadshows", but you can all share some of the fun and excitement with these photos of the first ever "Roadshow" when the Rollers topped the bill!

(Left) Sally and David and (above left) with the Rollers. The BCR's, as you can see, enjoyed themselves every bit as much as their fans, who helped them out with their pop quiz answers!

THE TOMORROW PEOPLE

PERHAPS THE MOST REMARKABLE THING ABOUT THE TOMORROW PEOPLE IS THEIR ABILITY TO JAUNT... TO TELEPORT THEIR BODIES OVER VAST DISTANCES IN THE BLINK OF AN EYE. AS WHEN JOHN AND ELIZABETH, HOLIDAYING IN THE WEST INDIES, RECEIVE AN URGENT TELEPATHIC MESSAGE FROM THEIR BIOTRONIC COMPUTER, TIM, BASED IN LONDON...

OH, OH! BACK WE GO! I MIGHT'VE KNOWN WE WOULDN'T GET A FULL FORTNIGHT OF PEACE AND QUIET!

I WONDER WHAT'S WRONG, NOW?

THE SLEEPY LOCALS HARDLY NOTICE THEIR DEPARTURE...

THEY FIND STEPHEN, TYSO AND MIKE ALREADY WITH TIM...

AREN'T WE THE SUMMERY ONES! LEFT YOUR LUGGAGE TO JAUNT ON ITS OWN, DID YOU?

YOU CAN JOLLY WELL GO AND COLLECT IT, FOR YOUR CHEEK.

WHAT'S UP, TIM?

YOU'VE HEARD OF PROFESSOR MAXIMILIAN DUCROS, JOHN? HE'S BEEN EXPERIMENTING FOR YEARS ON HIS OWN THEORIES OF TELEPORT-TRANSFERENCE...

OF COURSE. TRYING TO BECOME THE FIRST ORDINARY HUMAN TO JAUNT...

DON'T SAY HE'S DONE IT....!

TIM SAYS THAT HE MADE A STATEMENT YESTERDAY THAT HE WAS ON THE EDGE OF A MAJOR BREAKTHROUGH...

THEIR HEADQUARTERS BENEATH THE LONDON STREET IS SUDDENLY TENSE...

AND NOW—HE'S VANISHED! THE PEOPLE ON THE GALACTIC TRIG ARE WORRIED, JOHN. IF HE HAS DISCOVERED A WAY OF JAUNTING...

PHEW! YOU MEAN HE MIGHT HAVE BEEN SNATCHED—BY CROOKS. EVEN BY ALIENS!

IT MEANS A FAST INVESTIGATION! AS SENIORS, JOHN AND ELIZABETH GO TOGETHER, AND TAKE MIKE BELL WITH THEM...

POOH! DUCROS CERTAINLY DIDN'T BELIEVE IN KEEPING HIS GRASS CUT!

TYPICAL BOFFIN. LIVES FOR HIS RESEARCH. COME ON—LET'S GET INSIDE. YOUR JOB, MIKE.

JOHN M. BURNS.

26th June 1976 • Art: John M. Burns • Story: Angus Allan

Follow the drama on page 64

LOOK-IN ON THE TV STUDIO

A new game devised by Eric Linden.

WHAT AN EXCITING DAY this is going to be. It's the day when you can make a studio visit and maybe even win the jackpot on The Golden Shot. But first you have got to get to the studios, and that involves a trip to town. You have to obey all the instructions along the way and then carry on obeying instructions when you get into the studios themselves.

HOW TO PLAY:

Any number can play. Use a dice, or make yourself a spinner. Each player has one throw. Highest number starts.

Place counter on 'Your House' square to start. Square to the left of it will be the first one in the actual game.

Each player throws in turn. He must obey all the instructions on the squares he lands on. Any number may land on the same square without penalty. Throwing six does **NOT** give another throw.

If you have to go back you must still obey all the signs on the square where you finally land, no matter how many times you may already have been there.

SQUARES INSIDE HEAVY BLACK LINES

Each square shape inside heavy lines counts the same as the ordinary squares, so it would take 3 to get through the Follyfoot Farm; 2 to get through On The Buses and so on. But if you land on any square inside heavy outlined area you must obey the instruction.

You must land exactly on The Golden Shot to win. If you throw too many you must bounce back—and obey any instructions on square you return to.

The winner will be the first to get into The Golden Shot studio.

TO MAKE A SPINNER

Cut out the spinner carefully, and stick down on cardboard of the same shape. Push matchstick or cocktail stick through centre, and then your spinner will be complete.

CONGRATULATIONS! YOU'VE HIT THE JACKPOT ON THE GOLDEN SHOT, AND WON THE GAME!

LIFT OFF... SING AYSHEA BROUGH THE CHORUS OF ANY POP NUMBER, AND TAKE ANOTHER THROW. TOO SHY TO SING? RETURN TO RECEPTION

LOST YOUR WAY... GO BACK TO WORLD OF SPORT

LOST PASS.... RETURN TO RECEPTION FOR ANOTHER

MAKE-UP ROOM NOT FOR YOU. GO ON 3

YOU'VE TAKEN DR. WARING'S STETHOSCOPE, RETURN IT TO RECEPTION

CLAPPER-BOARD HAS LOST ITS FILM CLIPS

IMITATE ANY FILM STAR OR CARTOON CHARACTER AND GO ON 4, MISS A THROW IF YOU FAIL

MISTAKEN FOR ARTIST... RUSH BACK TO LIFT-OFF STUDIO

RESTAURANT... QUICK SERVICE, GO ON 2

NOTICES

STOP TO READ NOTICE-BOARD.. MISS TURN

DOCTOR IN CHARGE REHEARSAL... MIME SOMETHING ABOUT DOCTORS,

FIRST TO GUESS IT DOUBLES NEXT SCORE

NEED MAKE-UP AFTER ALL... GO THERE RIGHT AWAY

AUTOGRAPH ALBUM LEFT IN RESTAURANT GO BACK FOR IT

WORLD OF SPORT... NAME TWO SPORTING STARS, NOT ALREADY NAMED, FOR DICKIE TO CHAT ABOUT. ANOTHER THROW IF YOU CAN, MISS TURN IF YOU CAN'T

CANTEEN... ENJOY MEAL, MISS TURN

SUNDAY NIGHT AT THE LONDON PALLADIUM... CAUGHT IN REVOLVING STAGE... THROW ODD NUMBER BEFORE YOU CAN MOVE

FANCY A CUP OF TEA... GO TO CANTEEN FOR IT

STUDIO RECEPTION... WAIT HERE 'TIL YOU THROW AN ODD NUMBER

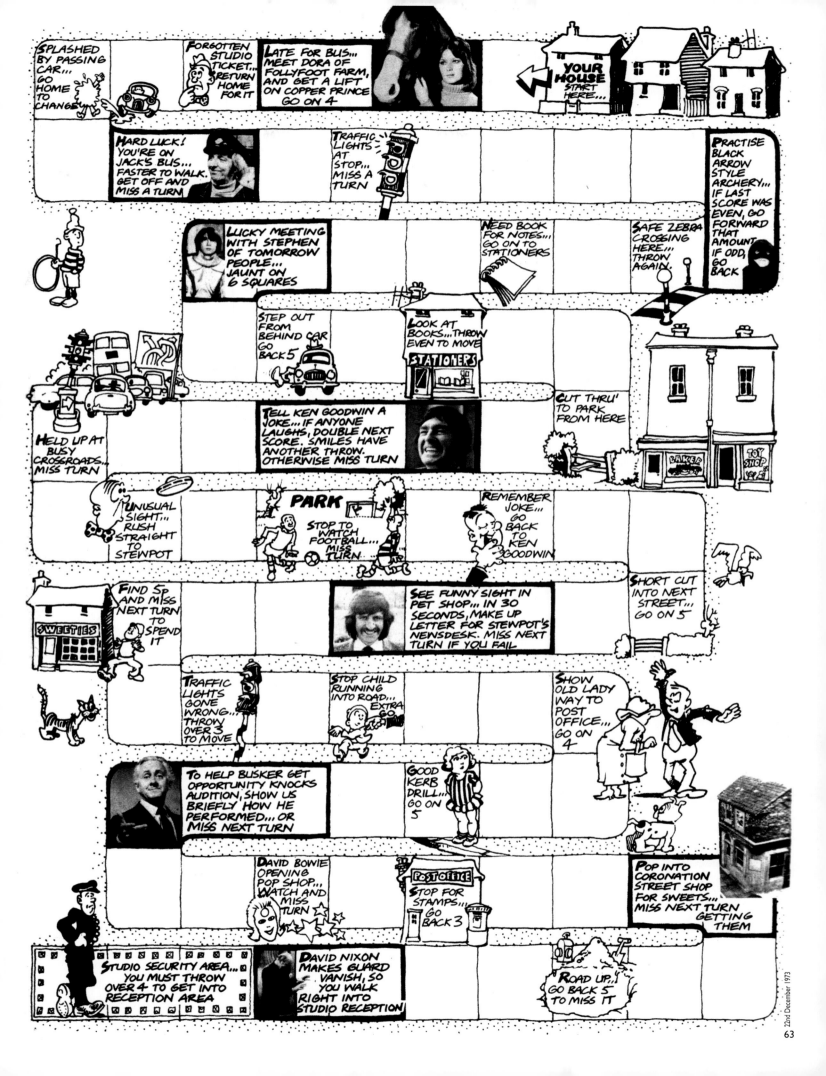

Who will volunteer? See page 68

****

Who will be the Look-in New World Young Cooks of the Year for 1975?

LOOK-IN/NEW WORLD YOUNG COOKS' CLUB
CHEF CAT

INTRODUCED BY KATHIE WEBBER COOKERY EDITOR OF TVTIMES

Fabulous competition open to ALL Look-in readers – £1,000 worth of prizes must be won!

The competition will be in three stages and will be judged in two age groups—6 to 11 years of age and 12 to 16 years, which means that there will be TWO "Young Cooks of the Year" for 1975. The prizes will be awarded as follows:

★ **£150** first prize to the winner of each age group

★ **£25** prize for each of the four runners-up in the final

★ **6** Raleigh cycles for the regional winners

★ **20** Polaroid colourpak 80 cameras for the regional runners-up

Regular readers will remember Dawn Hanley, the Look-in/New World Young Cook of the Year for 1974. Although Dawn's reign is not yet over, the time has come for us to start looking for next year's "Young Cooks of the Year". The competition is open to ALL

Dawn Hanley

Look-in readers between 6 and 16, which means boys as well as girls!

Entry is free and open to all Look-in readers in the two age groups living in the United Kingdom and as a special bonus all entrants will receive FREE membership of the Young Cooks' Club.

Should an existing member win any of the above prizes, he or she will receive an additional mystery prize.

THE THREE STAGES ARE AS FOLLOWS:

Stage 1. First you must enter the competition on the right hand page. You have to identify the six dishes shown and think up another name for the dish pictured on this page. From these entries, 13 from each age group will be chosen to enter the Regional Finals of which there will be three. A Northern Final (which will include Northern Ireland and the Isle of Man), a Midlands Final, and a Southern Final (which will include the Channel Islands). The closing date for receipt of entries is 30th November, 1974.

Macaroni Cheese

Stage 2. A " Cook-in " using NEW WORLD gas cookers will be held at the venues of the three regional finals during February of 1975. Each regional finalist will have to prepare the same set menu. The two age group winners from each of the three regional finals will go forward to a National Final to be held at Stratford-upon-Avon on 15th March, 1975.

Stage 3. Grand Final. A " Cook-in " will again be held, between the three finalists in each age group. Once again, each of the finalists will have to prepare a set menu to decide the two Look-in/New World " Young Cooks of the Year " for 1975.

****

1

2

3

4

5

6

TO ENTER this fabulous competition presented by the Look-in/New World Young Cooks' Club, you must first look at the pictured dishes above and then pair them off with the list of names printed next to the coupon. When you have done that and written your answers, together with your name, address, date of birth and club membership number, if a member, on the spaces provided on the coupon, look at the tie breaker picture on the opposite page. You will probably recognise it as macaroni cheese, but that's not what we want to know. We want you to think of another name for this popular dish. Should it be necessary, the tie breaker will be used to select the regional finalists, when, in the opinion of the appointed judges, the senders of the most suitable and original names will be selected. In all stages of the competition the editor's decision will be final and no correspondence can be entered into. All necessary travelling and accommodation expenses for regional finalists and grand finalists, together with one parent or guardian, will be met by NEW WORLD Gas Cookers Ltd.

A. Jam Turnovers
B. Stuffed Tomatoes
C. Tomato Soup with Croutons
D. Poor Knights of Windsor
E. Coley Fish Cakes
F. Upside-down pudding

Send to : Young Cooks Of The Year Competition, Look-in/New World Young Cooks' Club, P.O. Box 101, London, NW10 0JP.

Answers :

A ....   D...

B ....   E...

C ....   F...

My suggested name for the tie-break is ....

....

Membership Number (if already a member) ....

Name ....

Address ....

....

....

Date of birth ....
Closing date : November 30th, 1974.

Look-in/New World Young Cooks' Club is presented by arrangement with New World (Gas Cookers) Ltd.

An incredible experiment on John.

THE TOMORROW PEOPLE

PROFESSOR MAXIMILIEN DUCROS, EXPERIMENTING WITH A METHOD OF TELEPORT-TRANSFERENCE ('THE VAUNTING' THAT COMES NATURALLY TO THE TOMORROW PEOPLE) MISCALCULATES ON HIS THEORIES AND ENDS UP MINIATURISING HIMSELF TO LITTLE MORE THAN TWO INCHES IN HEIGHT! AND WHEN THE TOMORROW PEOPLE THEMSELVES DISCOVER WHAT HAS HAPPENED...

WE KNOW HE'S SOMEWHERE BENEATH US...IN A MOUSE'S TUNNEL, OF ALL THINGS! HE MAY BE INJURED...AT THE *LEAST* HE'LL BE TERRIFIED...

AND THERE'S ONLY *ONE* WAY TO GET HIM BACK TO SAFETY!

YES. ONE OF US HAS TO REPEAT THE EXPERIMENT. ONE OF *US* HAS TO SHRINK DOWN TO HIS SIZE AND GO IN AFTER HIM!

FIRST, A QUICK TELEPATHIC QUERY TO TIM, THEIR BIOTRONIC COMPUTER...

YES, JOHN. FROM WHAT YOU TELL ME OF THE EXPERIMENTAL SET-UP, THE PROCESS *CAN* BE REVERSED. BUT REMEMBER— THE DANGERS CONFRONTING A TWO-INCH MAN ARE UNBOUNDED!

JOHN'S SENIORITY CANCELS ALL ARGUMENT ABOUT WHO IS TO BE THE GUINEA-PIG...

READY, JOHN...?

GO AHEAD, MIKE!

THA-RASSA!

SKRAAKKK!

IT'S UNCANNY! HOW—HOW DO YOU FEEL?

WELL—ODD, BUT OKAY, I RECKON...

INCREDIBLY, NEXT INSTANT...

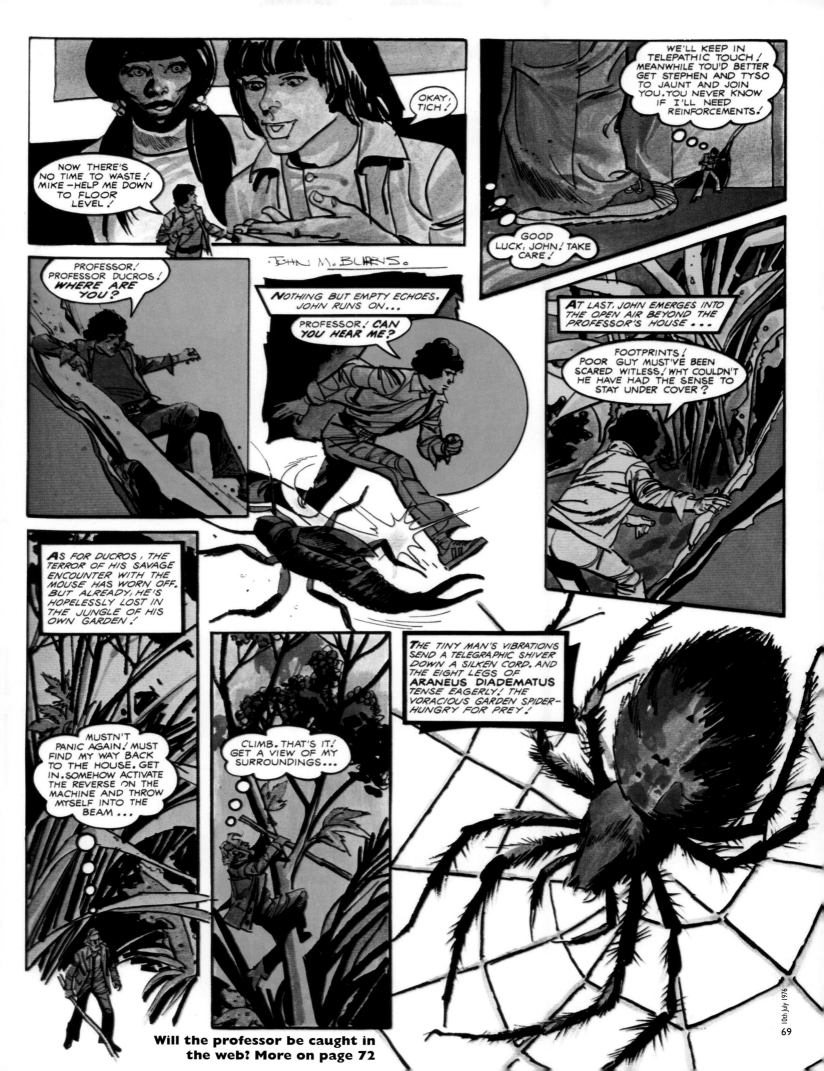

Will the professor be caught in
the web? More on page 72

DOCTOR WHO'S ENEMIES ARE FREE!

4-free full-colour stand-up figures inside every Doctor Who pack of Weetabix. With a free action setting on the back of every pack. In all there are six different Daleks to collect and two colourful figures of the Doctor. Then there's Sarah Jane, the Giant Robot, Cyberman, Sea Devil and a dozen more terrific monsters and robots. Plus six different action settings. And on some packs there's a fabulous full-colour cut-out model of the Tardis. So dig into your time traveller's breakfast and journey into outer space.

HAVE **YOU** HAD YOUR DAILY WHEAT?

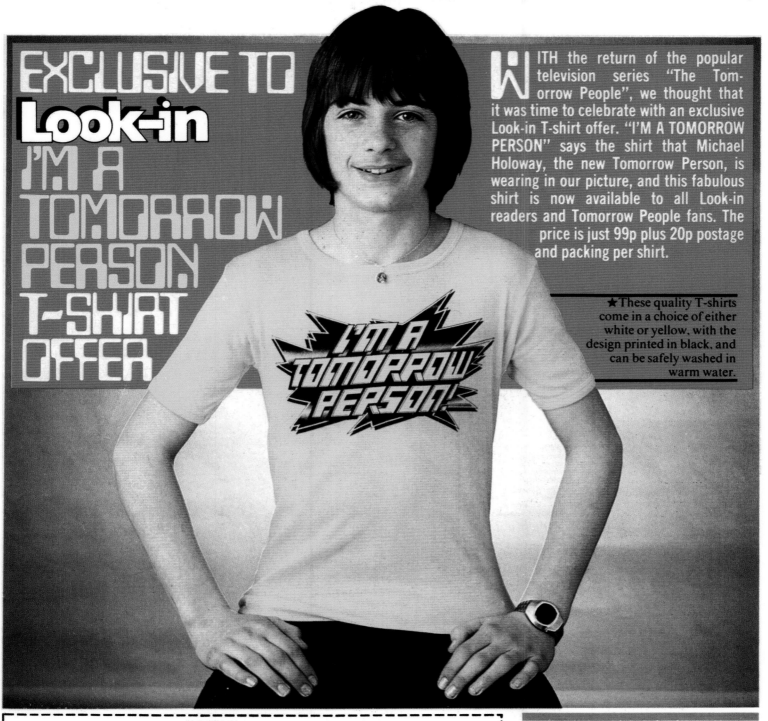

EXCLUSIVE TO Look-in
I'M A TOMORROW PERSON T-SHIRT OFFER

WITH the return of the popular television series "The Tomorrow People", we thought that it was time to celebrate with an exclusive Look-in T-shirt offer. "I'M A TOMORROW PERSON" says the shirt that Michael Holoway, the new Tomorrow Person, is wearing in our picture, and this fabulous shirt is now available to all Look-in readers and Tomorrow People fans. The price is just 99p plus 20p postage and packing per shirt.

★These quality T-shirts come in a choice of either white or yellow, with the design printed in black, and can be safely washed in warm water.

Total No. of T-shirts required: ☐
Sizes: write totals required of each chest size in boxes below:

Yellow with black print

22	24	26	28/30	32/34	34/36	36/38
☐	☐	☐	☐	☐	☐	☐

White with black print

22	24	26	28/30	32/34	34/36	36/38
☐	☐	☐	☐	☐	☐	☐

Send to: LOOK-IN T-SHIRT OFFER, P.O. Box 30, Sidcup, DA14 4PG, Kent.

I enclose a cheque/p.o. no. ....
.... for ....
made payable to ITV Publications Limited.

Write clearly with BLOCK LETTERS only

Name ....

Address ....

....

Postcode ....
Please allow 21 days for delivery.

HOW TO ORDER

You may order as many T-shirts as you like, at a cost of 99p plus 20p postage and packing per shirt, but please state on the order form the following points:

(a) The total number of T-shirts required;
(b) The total number of each chest size of T-shirt required of each colour;
(c) The total sum of money enclosed;
(d) Your name and address in BLOCK LETTERS, please.

Send ONLY cheques or postal orders — DO NOT SEND MONEY THROUGH THE POST. All cheques and postal orders must be made payable to ITV Publications Ltd., and crossed. Send to: LOOK-IN T-SHIRT OFFER, P.O. Box 30, Sidcup, DA14 4PG, Kent.

13th March 1976

KRAKK!

Frightened by the attack, the spider beats a hasty retreat...

MMMFF!

Quickly, Professor! Before something else turns up! Get down and join me!

We know your research is sponsored by the Galactic Trig, Professor... but you shouldn't have taken such a chance with theoretical equipment...

He's got him!

And we've got a telepathic fix on their position! We can guide 'em in safely!

I know that now! Thank goodness they put you tomorrow people on to me...

It'd have been awkward if you'd been a complete outsider, unaware of our powers... but don't worry, you're quite safe now, and the ray can be reversed!

Yes, within moments, we'll be back to our normal selves...

And then - the totally unforeseen! From way up above, a gimlet-eyed sparrowhawk drops like a thunderbolt! Without the slightest breath of warning...

AAARGH! GARRGH!

KLOMMMP!

Follow the drama on page 82

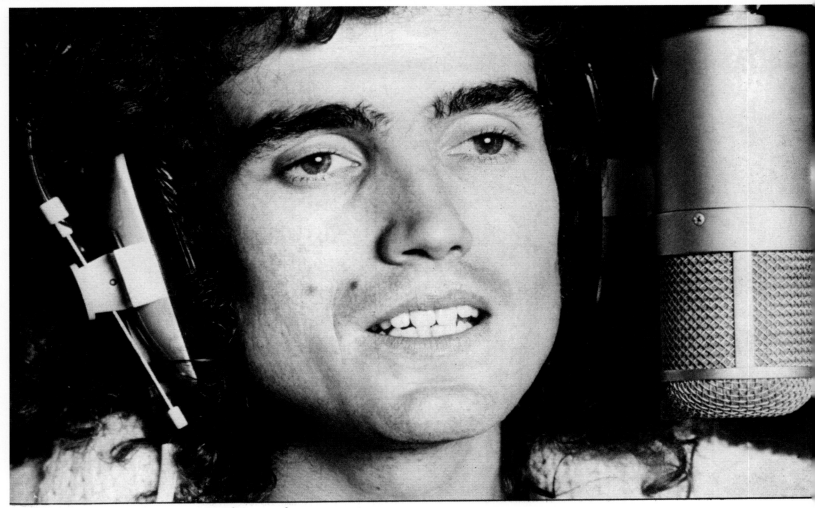

Look-in on... MICK'S MUSIC

WE JOIN MICK ROBERTSON IN THE RECORDING STUDIO AS HE MAKES HIS FIRST ALBUM.

Magpie's trendy young presenter, Mick Robertson, has had two of the happiest and most eventful years of his life. Upon leaving college his ambition was to be a school teacher but now Mick has become a household face and an idol of females from six to sixty. Before entering teaching, Mick decided to work with a children's television programme gathering experience that would help him reach the youngsters that much easier. During the college holidays he had a spell working with a parks play scheme for children and he also chose to do a project for children's television, thereby making himself some very useful contacts. He heard of a job as a background researcher with the twice weekly magazine programme 'Magpie', and the rest is now history. From a background researcher to a frontline presenter. Mick has performed many exciting and often dangerous activities on the programme but has always enjoyed it tre-

mendously, although he has had this to say:

"I hate heights, and they are forever getting me to perch up on high places or to be rescued from the top of a cliff. I even flew one of those huge kites that you hang from—I messed it up and really hurt my back."

Surely the nicest thing that has happened to Mick since joining 'Magpie' is his venture into the music business.

"As long as I can remember," says Mick, "I have always wanted to make a record and having 'The Tango's Over' released was a fantasy come true!"

Tango was not the biggest hit of the year although it did reach number fifty-three in the charts. In fact it made Mick one of the most successful newcomers to the pop-business for it is very rare that a singer's first record makes the charts. Since the 'Tango' Mick has made an album and another single. The L.P., which is en-➤➤➤➤➤

titled 'Then I Changed Hands', will be on release around Christmas and features Mick singing everything from rock to blues.

The actual making of the album proved to be an eye-opener for him. All the backing tracks were recorded before he even entered the studios to record his vocals. An 'orchestra' of twenty-four session musicians, under the direction of Richard Hewson, the writer, arranger and producer of the L.P., were brought together and the various backing tracks recorded. It's not an easy job singing on an album for it requires an enormous amount of vocal power and that can very easily lead to temporary loss of voice. With some songs the first attempt or 'take' will be acceptable. On other songs it may require five or six 'takes' to get it exactly right. "To record the album took me about thirty hours, which I am told is about normal."

Before the album is ready for sale it has to be pressed and mixed. 'Mixing' means that the backing tracks have to blend with Mick's voice to produce just the correct sound. The job of balancing was done by Nick Sykes—the engineer. Using a sixteen track recorder and the mixer, Nick spent many hours along with Richard Hewson till the best possible results had been achieved.

Despite the fact that Mick was also very busy with his Magpie commitments he obviously enjoyed making the album and even found time to write the lyrics for two of the songs—one of which, 'Then I Changed Hands' is both the title track and the follow-up single.

"I am enjoying myself so much I just don't seem to get tired," says Mick. "It has the same effect on me as Magpie—the more I work the more I seem to enjoy it."

Mick has proved himself to be a unique character within children's television. He dresses casually but smartly, has long curly hair and looks every inch a pop star. Mick can communicate with youngsters and youngsters dig Mick. He has a bright future ahead of him on television and on the pop scene.

Richard Hewson (left), Mick, and engineer Nick Sykes.

"How do you drive this thing?"

75

+++MESSAGE ORIGIN: MOONBASE ALPHA—SPACE+++
+++MESSAGE TIMED: 1999+++

+++YOU—YES, **YOU**, READER—HAVE CEASED TO EXIST+++FOR ALL WE KNOW, YOU PERISHED IN THE FIRST DAYS OF TURMOIL THAT FOLLOWED BREAKAWAY +++YOUR EXACT FATE WILL NEVER BE KNOWN TO US, FOR WE ARE THE WANDERERS+++THE LAST MEMBERS OF OUR GREAT CIVILISATION, DOOMED TO VOYAGE SPACE, PERHAPS FOR AN ETERNITY OF GENERATIONS, LOOKING FOR A NEW EARTH, A NEW HOME+++

IT HAPPENED on September 9, 1999. The Moon — *our* Moon — home of a vast scientific complex known as Moonbase Alpha, shuddered to the multiple blasts of mounting nuclear explosion as dump after dump of buried radioactive waste became live and heated beyond endurance.

Was it the result of some sinister alien force? That question cannot be answered — and now, with the Moon torn bodily from Earth's orbit, the answer is of no consequence. For Moonbase and its personnel, miraculously unscathed in the fearful holocaust, survival is the only thing that matters. Powerless to direct their course, they face the dangers, the hopes, the fears of a journey through the uncharted universe — into the depths of the unknown!

This, then, is the background to ITC's new and gripping Sci-fi series, *Space 1999* — the product of the fertile minds of Gerry and Sylvia Anderson, who gave us the masterpiece of *Thunderbirds* and *Captain Scarlet*, action ranging from the puppetry of *Supercar* to live filming of *UFO*. And this, their latest dazzling adventure, crammed with the ultimate in spectacular visual effects, continues the live-action format that began after *Joe 90*.

Martin Landau, of *Mission —*

Impossible fame, plays Commander John Koenig, Commander of the Moonbase. His wife Barbara Bain plays his medical supremo, Doctor Helena Russell. Barry Morse (Inspector Gerard from the long-running *Fugitive* series) stars in the role of scientist Professor Victor Bergman. And week by week, top acting names come to guest in this fascinating drama of mounting tension that takes us into the mind-boggling future!

You — yes, *you*, reader — will ride the flight deck of the Moonbase Eagle craft. Will explore the surfaces of hostile planets hitherto unseen by the eye of man. Will see the incredible effects of unguessed dimensions in space that make a mockery of time as we know it. Both on TV and in Look-in, Space 1999 is an odyssey beyond the limits of human experience.

The explosion (top) that caused the Moon to break away from the Earth's orbit. (Above) Roving about the Nuclear Waste Dump on Moonbase Alpha.

Torn towards an unknown future — left to right Professor Bergman (Barry Morse), Dr Helena Russell (Barbara Bain) and Commander Koenig (Martin Landau)

An Eagle shuttlecraft prepares to investigate an alien spaceship.

Commander Koenig (played by Martin Landau) reaches for the heavens

An eerie stranger infiltrates Moonbase Alpha.

THE SATURDAY SPECTACULARS!

Sally James — recording artist.

The topic of conversation (below) is a didgeridoo, and in the picture with Sally are Rolf Harris and Stewpot.

ARE YOU one of the lucky viewers in the London Weekend and ATV areas who avidly watch the Saturday Morning "specials" — 'Saturday Scene' and 'Tiswas'? If not, then make a date with your alarm clock, and set it for 9.40 if you're in the London area, and 10.10 if you're a Midlander.

Readers from other regions have every reason to feel envious, for 'Saturday Scene' and 'Tiswas' are very popular indeed, combining different and exciting features into their healthy Saturday morning slot.

'Tiswas' is introduced by John Asher and Chris Tarrant, assisted by Peter Tomlinson, ATV's weekend station announcer. He has to bear the brunt of their gags and jokes, but keeps coming back for more!

London viewers, meanwhile, have the weekly bonus of being able to focus their eyes on attractive Sally James, presenter of 'Saturday Scene,' and singer to boot! Sally, who has released a single, is herself in constant touch with musicians, who always feature prominently as guests on the programme.

The basic difference between the two productions is that 'Saturday Scene,' although having its fair share of readers' requests and letters, relies heavily on programme content, whereas 'Tiswas' is basically made for its viewers — by its viewers. For instance, each week there are competitions for over 8 year olds and under 8 year olds. A sports item, introduced by Trevor East, relies on viewers' requests for its content, as do the many film clips that are shown each week. Viewers who send in requests to the programme participate in its special "private telephone number." Those whose letters are to be used on the show receive a call from ATV and are able to phone-in on the number that only they are given. No other viewers know it — and so only the lucky ones can make use of it.

'Tiswas' is a lot of fun; its viewer participation makes it quite unique on television.

On 'Saturday Scene' the accent is on excitement and adventure, and every week features the bubbling pop sounds of '45' and

22nd March 1975

'45' DJ Kid Jensen.

jungle drama with 'Tarzan.' One of the programmes incorporated in the 'Scene' is 'London Bridge,' which is a magazine-type show aimed at viewers aged from 11-16. It's introduced by Michael Wale, whom many of you will know as a DJ on Radio One, but perhaps not so many of you will know is also a regular contributor in the Queens Park Rangers match-day programme!

Pop fans watching last week's 'London Bridge' will have seen the Bay City Rollers, while this Saturday (the 22nd) it's the turn of cinema buffs to be treated, for director Ken Russell is on the show, looking at films by young amateurs and giving advice as to how their work could be improved.

Readers' letters, as on 'Tiswas,' are a regular feature of 'Saturday Scene,' and Sally James also reviews her 'Tips For The Top' in the pop world, and ends each week with the number one sound.

Well, that's a basic run-down of the two Saturday morning spectaculars in London and the Midlands. It's more than likely whet the appetite of many a Look-in reader in other parts of the country . . . so come on then, write to us, telling us whether or not you'd like to have your own Saturday morning programme, and for those who *do* watch 'Saturday Scene' and 'Tiswas' let's have your views, too. Send your opinions to 'Saturday Show,' Look-in, 247, Tottenham Court Road, London, W1P 0AU.

crazy moment from 'Tiswas', with (left to right): Peter Tomlinson, John Asher and Chris Tarrant.

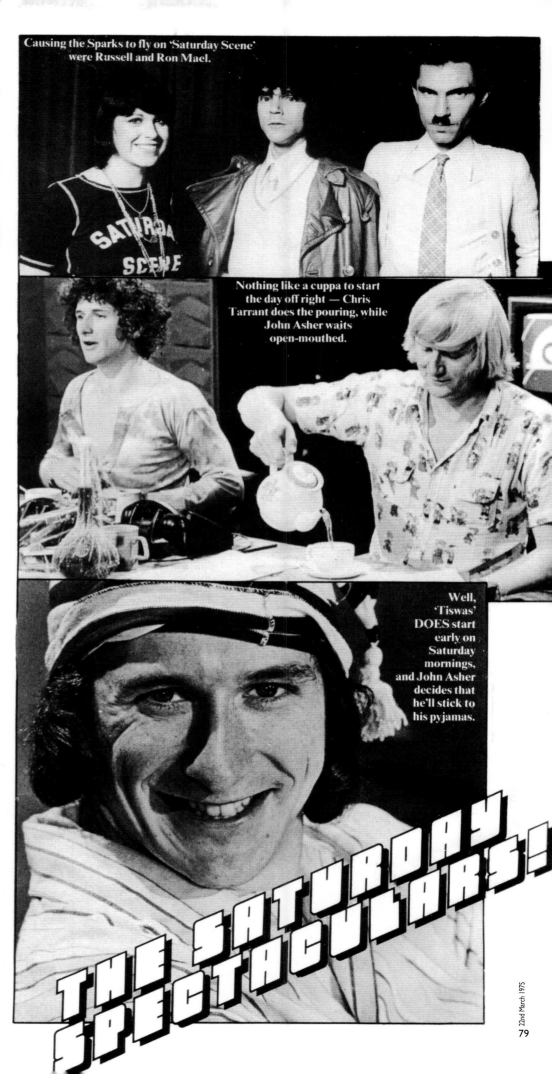

Causing the Sparks to fly on 'Saturday Scene' were Russell and Ron Mael.

Nothing like a cuppa to start the day off right — Chris Tarrant does the pouring, while John Asher waits open-mouthed.

Well, 'Tiswas' DOES start early on Saturday mornings, and John Asher decides that he'll stick to his pyjamas.

THE SATURDAY SPECTACULARS!

POP QUEST

Each week in "Pop Quest", we take a look at the charts, at the screen, and into the past to come up with lots of pop posers for you. If you're stuck on some, brothers and sisters, aunts and uncles and even Mums and Dads might surprise you with their pop knowledge, so try asking them, too. . .

★★★★★★★★★★★★★★

(1) Dan McCafferty had a hit with his single "Out Of Time" recently. Can you name the artist who released the original version and first had a hit with it about ten years ago?

(2) Talking of Dan McCafferty, do you know with which band he sings, and their last Top Twenty hit?

(3) Which group does "The Duke" belong to?

(4) Can you name the artist who had a hit with "Motor Biking"?

(5) Which American female trio was once led by Diana Ross? (They're pictured here).

SLEEVE SPOT

(6) Can you identify this album (with the give-away lettering deleted?)

(7) Disco Tex (below) is an amazing person! Do you know his nationality and another of his names?

ANAGRAM

(8) Can you rearrange this name to spell out a top singer?
DARIL VASTNUTS

(9) Lovely Luan Peters sings with the group 5000 Volts (below) who had a big hit with "I'm On Fire". Luan is, however, better known as an actress. Can you name the top Granada television series that she once appeared in?

(10) Can you name Mud's new man and the instrument that he plays? (He's with them below).

25th October 1975

11 Do you know which star was planning to live next door to Elton John in Beverley Hills . . . until his house burned down before he even moved in?

14 Can you name the man who had a big hit with Summertime City?

12 The Rollers recently released a single in the States. Do you know which one?

15 Complete the missing words from these groups:

   . . . And The Sunshine Band
   . . . Knight And The Pips
   . . . Corporation
   Kool And The . . .

13 Alvin Stardust spent his childhood in Mansfield, but do you know where he was born?

16 Roger Daltrey (below) of The Who scored a big hit in "Tommy". Lately he's been making a film about an entirely different character — but who is it?

17 Labelle, the all-girl trio, (above) had a hit with "Lady Marmalade". Do you know what Labelle used to be called?

18 Average White Band now live in America, but they weren't born there. Do you know from which country they hail?

19 Can you name Cilla Black's husband?

20 Below you see a pretty unlikely pair of rather muddy footballers! Do you recognise them?

More tense action on page 86

MUD MOVE ON SEZ LES

⬤ We felt that seven singles last year and three albums was a bit silly; it was saturation of the market ⬤

THOSE words came from Mud front-man Les Gray, and that's why we haven't heard from the boys for a few months. They've been taking time out to recharge the batteries and have succeeded very nicely indeed with their new single "Shake It Down". Les spoke recently to Look-in's Richard Tippett. "We needed a break and a re-think about what we were doing. In the singles market you can't go on in one direction as long as we've being going on. You've got to move it around a bit, and try and give people variation. We wanted to develop something a little bit more individual, which we've done."

It's a funky, disco-type single — certainly a new road for Mud to travel down. Did Rob Davies and Ray Stiles write it with a disco audience in mind? "Yeah, I think so," replied Les. "We tend to watch people a lot, and what people are getting into. It was a natural progression really. Most of the stuff we've done in the past has been dancing material relative to the time it was released. It's been "in vogue". When we go to discotheques now we look around and think: 'Ah, that's what everyone's dancing to at the moment'. And so consequently Rob and Ray were influenced by that. The song didn't sound like it does now when they first started writing it. It was much slower. But it developed, with the disco feel right to the fore."

Have the group got a new album on the way? Mud Rockers anxiously await the first 1976 offering from the foursome. **"We've just been talking about it today,"** ⟫⟫⟫

said Les. "Originally, we had been only contracted for one album. But our new record company were very pleased with the first one we did for them, and I've just found out that they've agreed to go ahead and finance another one. We've got a few tracks already that we've recorded.

"There'll be all sorts of things on the LP. The album songs we write tend not to follow the same pattern."

Mud have recently done the European rounds, and Les was quick to commend their reception in different countries. Beginning with a concert in Belgium. "It was absolutely amazing. It was at a huge arena in Antwerp, and it was really packed out. I remember thinking: 'There can't be another gig like that', but then we played Germany, where we hadn't gone down too well before, and we played to thousands and thousands of people. It was great, and I thought: 'Well, that was tremendous'. Then we moved on to Poland, and I was a bit terrified. But one night we played two shows in a place called Lodz, with

'I may do something on my own as a little extra... a fun solo album'

7,000 fans at each house. They wanted us to do a third show!

"So you can never really pick out one particular venue that you've enjoyed more than any other.

"We've just been to East Germany where we met the top Russian band, who have apparently sold twenty million records in Russia. They intend to cover some of our songs, and in time we should be going over to Moscow for concerts."

So it's all go for Mud. But is it 'all go' for any more of Les's Elvis Presley take-offs on record? "No, not with Mud," laughed Les.

"It's possible that, later on in the year, if there's time to fit it in, I may do something on my own as a little extra. It would be a fun solo album. It would be a bonus to get into, and would more than likely be a rock 'n' roll-type thing, because Mud as a group is moving on from that, but a lot of people still like it.

"The Elvis thing wasn't calculated at all. I started to take off Presley after I had been trying to bring off a lot of different voices and expressions in the studio to get a bit more into the songs."

Well, Les has got into more than that Elvis's vocal style. He's acted for the cinema, recorded a Green Cross Code advert at Hammersmith — and, if you know Hammersmith, you'll appreciate that's no easy matter — and he's also taken to speedway (Mud are all supporters of the Wimbledon Speedway Club).

But, more important than anything else, Les and the group are still turning out the hits, with **Shake It Down** shaking it up the charts, where the boys belong!

Mud wheeling their way to more success!

31st July 1976

THE WORLDS OF GERRY ANDERSON

You may recall that I told you about my exciting exhibition called 'Gerry Anderson's Space City' **on this page recently. Well, the exhibition is now in full swing at Blackpool's Golden Mile Centre, and is open every day throughout the summer, admission 20p.**

There have been some very flattering comments about the many items on display. These include many of Brian Johnson's magnificent models (such as Eagles, Thunderbirds and Lady Penelope's car), lots of costumes and special effects props, behind-the-scenes filming plans (you can see how a scene in **Space 1999** is worked out), and there is also a huge model of an Eagle made out of Meccano, part of an interesting display which shows the step by step production of the Dinky Toys' Eagle.

We have arranged a special Look-in display, too, which includes original Space 1999 artwork from Look-in and introduces our picture strip writer Angus Allan and the two artists who drew the strips, Michael Noble and John Burns.

There is much, much more, including the best designs that you submitted to the Look-in 'Space City' competition.

(Below) It's all happening at 'Gerry Anderson's Space City'. Why not pay it a visit?

**Catherine Schell
as Maya**
Space:1999

Annual 1977

Have you seen these great Look-in Books?

Joining the wide range of Look-in Books are four brand new titles, packed with interest and entertainment . . .

THE FLOCKTON FLYER

Peter Whitbread

Based on the Southern Television series, this is the story of The Flyer, painstakingly restored by 'The Flockton And Lane End Railway Preservation Society', which means mainly by Bob Carter and his family, who all move into an old station. The adventures include coming to the rescue of a circus when fire breaks out, saving sheep stranded on a cliff in a snowstorm, organising a Christmas special, and finally opening the line with the help of six shire horses . . .

THE ROLF HARRIS ANIMAL QUIZ BOOK

Roy Harris

How do mice eat frozen meat? How do hedgehogs catch live birds and animals? What happens when two shrews meet? These and over 300 other intriguing questions are posed and answered in this fascinating illustrated book covering all the animals to be found in the British Isles and you can also find out how to observe the animals in their natural habitat.

MAGPIE MAKE AND DO

Eileen Deacon

Eileen Deacon is a regular contributor to Magpie, and she includes here 27 different fun items to make — for boys as well as girls — some easy (like pebble people and decorated candles), others more challenging like a 1920's flapper doll. There are over fifty illustrations, and, where necessary, actual size patterns and step-by-step pictures are also included.

RUNAROUND QUIZ BOOK

Robin May

Roll up, roll up for over 400 questions like: Who was the first Doctor Who? Which dog has a blue tongue? Where would you meet a vampire bat?, each with three possible answers to choose from, just like the show. There are some great illustrations, too!

Published by Arrow/Independent Television Books Ltd.

Cooking can be great fun — especially if you're renowned for being an expert at it! Here, in an exclusive interview, Kathie Webber talks to . . . RICHARD O'SULLIVAN, food fanatic from Robin's Nest . . .

Serving up a tasty dish — that's Richard O'Sullivan

Following the success of Robin's Nest, in which Richard played the part of restaurateur Robin Tripp, I wanted to ask him how much of the cooking bit *is* acting. Can he really cook as he's supposed to in the series?

"Well," he said, "I can do roasts. I don't make sauces and stuff like that. I like simple tasty foods best. Good fish and chips, curries, a good takeaway Chinese.

"A lot of people don't cook for themselves but love to cook for others. I'm a pig and can do a whole roast for myself. I can quite easily go home and cook a stew or casserole for five and eat the lot — breakfast, tea, lunch, dinner. Robin is more into sauces but I prefer the traditional English bit because I like to taste the meat." But Richard does put garlic with his roasts and says he reeks of it. Not true. "I'd have garlic with my boiled eggs in the morning," he said. "I like it so much."

When people are invited to dinner at Richard's home, "they either like roasts or casseroles or they don't come round; it's as simple as that. One silly afternoon I had about 15 people all from the Man About The House series and it was chaos but great fun. It started at two in the afternoon and finished with coffees at about three in the morning — a good lunch."

Robin's Nest must be one of the nicest series for the technicians and camera crew to work on — they must queue to get the chance at eating all the food that's left over at the end of a day's shooting. "They love it," Richard said. "And so does the chef at the Thames TV restaurant. He's the one who prepares all the food for each day. He's told about a week in advance what's required in the script and he's getting the chance to try his hand at something different. And I like it, too," Richard continued. "I'm learning all kinds of new things to try at home." Here's Richard's recipe for his own Spaghetti Bolognaise and Pommes Lyonnaises . . .

SPAGHETTI BOLOGNAISE

1 medium onion
1oz. dripping
lb. minced beef
15oz. can tomatoes
good pinch dried basil
8oz. spaghetti

Skin and chop the onion. Heat the dripping in a large saucepan and add the onion. Fry for five minutes until the onion is soft, then stir in the mince and brown well. Season with salt and pepper and stir in the tomatoes and their juice. Add the basil and bring the mixture to the boil. Lower the heat and simmer the sauce for 30 min. Cook the spaghetti in a large pan of boiling salted water for about 15 min. or until the spaghetti is cooked but not soft and squashy. If you press a bit between your fingers, you should feel a slight resistance there. Drain well, put in a large serving dish and top with the Bolognaise sauce. Serve with Parmesan cheese to sprinkle on top. **Serves 4.**

POMMES LYONNAISES

1-1½lb. potatoes
salt and pepper
2 medium onions
3 tablespoons oil
1oz. butter
chopped parsley

Wash and peel the potatoes and cook them in boiling salted water for 15 to 20 min. until just tender. Drain and cut them into thin slices. Skin and slice the onions, then separate them into rings. Heat the oil and butter together in a large frying pan and fry the onions for 10 min. until golden brown. Drain and keep hot on a plate. Add the potatoes to the pan (you might need to add a little more oil and butter at this stage) and fry them for 10 to 15 min. until golden, turning them from time to time in the pan to make sure they brown evenly. Add the onions and cook together for 2 min. Season with salt and pepper and serve sprinkled with parsley. **Serves 4.**

22nd January 1977 • Art: Bill Titcombe • Story: Angus P. Allan

OUR KID ARE O.K!

Since Our Kid took "New Faces" by storm with an amazing 118 points out of 120, I've always wondered what they're really like. So when I found out that they were singing at a club near me, I went along to find out for myself.

To do this I spent the whole evening in their dressing room chatting to them and watching the atmosphere building as they got ready to go on stage.

While the boys were settling down I talked to their manager Francis Davies — the man who created Our Kid. I asked him why we hadn't been hearing so much of the lads lately. He explained: "We've had a lot of trouble with the school authorities. They said that the lads were spending too much time entertaining and not enough time studying. They made us cancel a lot of shows and T.V. work. This hurt us all very much as the boys had so much going for them." Fortunately, the two eldest members of the group left school at Easter. "This gives us much more freedom in planning.

"Now we can promote their new records and we will be back on screen again. We're also discussing an Our Kid series for television."

I asked the group how they combined being pop stars with life at home and at school in Liverpool. "We rehearse for two hours, three nights a week," Kevin told me. "Then, of course, there's all the time we spend actually performing. Our Mums and Dads are taking things in their stride and our schoolfriends are pretty cool about the whole thing." While the group all have other friends of their own ages, they get on very well together. "The only thing we quarrel about is what we watch on television!" said Brian.

NOW Francis comes back into the room and tells them to get a move-on. They will soon be due on stage, so they start to scramble into their suits. It's all very hectic. The compere is arranging the introduction, Francis is working out the running order and someone is trying to do a radio interview. I ask them if they're nervous, "Not really," says Terry McCreith. "The time we got really scared was when we did a concert at the Empire Theatre in Liverpool. We were terrified. It was the first time since the Beatles played there that they had to seal off London Road and Lime Street. They brought in extra police and there were 15 ambulances waiting outside. There was so much screaming that we could hardly hear ourselves. In the excitement one girl even jumped off the balcony!"

Everything is ready now. The lights go down and Kevin fumbles with his crutches. "I can't go on with these!" "You can do anything when you really want to," replies Francis firmly. There is a fanfare and Our Kid are on stage. They go straight into a real rocker called "Dance" and show that they are even better live than on record. The whole act is pure magic. Kevin's crutches are propped up against an amplifier. With a display of real guts, he sings and dances through the whole show. Seven more numbers and two encores later, the club echoes with cheers and we dash back into the dressing room. While the lads are getting changed, they sign photographs for the fans who are trying to push their way in. It's all part of a night's work for Our Kid.

When, at last, things cool down, the boys are brought some chips and more drinks. The subject of the conversation is their being mobbed. "Remember that time on the train when we had to lock ourselves in the toilet 'til we were given the all-clear?" asked Terry Baccino. "And the time those girls grabbed my jacket so I had to slip out of it before I could escape?" laughed Terry McCreith. "The worst thing was when they climbed in through Kev's bedroom window and stole his socks," said Brian. "But I wasn't in bed at the time," Kevin was quick to point out. "It's O.K. being mobbed in a big way, but I don't like the way I get followed and people hang around my home." I asked them if they had ever regretted going into show business. "Never," said Terry Baccino. "The only thing that has got me down is all this trouble with the schools. Normally if you leave school at my age you just don't stand a chance of getting a job. But although I've got a good one waiting for me with Our Kid, the education people don't seem to be too keen on the idea. But it's getting much better now that Terry and I are leaving school. We're looking forward to topping the bill in a summer season at Morecambe, and our new single came out recently. We've an L.P. lined up for release late in July, too. With all that and the "New Faces" gala final we're really getting into gear again."

Richard Howells

You've seen them recently on your TV screens - Now meet Our Kid...

TERRY McCREITH
Terry McCreith is the boistrous comedian of the group. He's 16 and takes charge of them when they're on stage. He says that his pet hate is people who pretend to be something they're not. He's very proud of his new guitar which he's tuning up ready for his solo spot in the show.

BRIAN FARRELL
The shy one is Brian Farrell and he's 14. Well — he seemed shy at first, but as the evening wore on he turned out to be quite a character, using Kevin's crutches as though they were machine guns. He's a Queen fan, and he hopes to see Liverpool win the European Cup.

TERRY BACCINO
Terry Baccino is 16 and seems to be the leading musician of the group. He's intelligent, straight-talking and sincere. He is a peaceful person and says that his ambition is: "To be happy and make other people happy."

KEVIN ROWAN
13-year-old Kevin Rowan curls up like a fieldmouse in the corner of the room. He's just had an operation on his toes and has to hobble about on crutches. Kevin is the group's lead singer and he's mad about sport. At school his favourite subjects are History and French.

BJORN GOT TO CHANGE, LUCKILY, BEFORE THAT NIGHT'S BANQUET. NEXT DAY, A CHAMPAGNE BREAKFAST AT A BRIGHTON HOTEL...

CORNFLAKES AND BUBBLY! WHAT A COMBINATION!

SOUNDS LIKE A GOOD TITLE FOR A SONG!

The New Viking Invasion

SWEDES SWEEP THE BOARD

ABBA ZOOM FROM SEVENTEEN TO NUMBER ONE

THE PRESS HAD PREVIOUSLY CALLED THEM OUTSIDERS...BUT NOW THEY DID THEM PROUD!

DAILY EXPRESS: AN ATTRACTIVE GROUP. AN IMMENSELY STRONG GROUP.

DAILY MAIL: FIRST TIME A POP GROUP WITH A DISCOTHEQUE SOUND HAS WON THE CONTEST...

IT WAS BACK TO SWEDEN AS NATIONAL HEROES AND HEROINES...BUT UNHAPPILY, THERE WAS GLOOM ON THE HORIZON! BEFORE THE CONTEST, THEY'D COMMITTED THEMSELVES TO A MONTH'S TOUR OF THE SWEDISH PARKS...

WE'VE HAD TO CANCEL. WE'RE NEEDED INTERNATIONALLY NOW. BUT OUR HOME PEOPLE ARE CALLING US TURNCOATS. THEY CONDEMN US FOR TURNING OUR BACKS ON OUR FANS HERE...

STIG—WE'D BE EXHAUSTED IF WE WENT AHEAD WITH THE TOUR! THEY MUST UNDERSTAND...

ABBA? TRAITORS IF YOU ASK ME! WE VOTED THEM IN FOR THE SONG CONTEST...

AND AS SOON AS THEY WIN, THEY TURN THEIR BACKS ON US! I'LL NEVER BUY ANY MORE OF THEIR RECORDS!

BUT TIME HAS A WAY OF SMOOTHING OVER THE HARDEST PROBLEMS. SOON ENOUGH, ATTITUDES CHANGED...

I SEE ABBA ARE BACK NEXT WEEK. ABOUT TIME, EH?

AH, BUT THEY'VE BEEN BUSY ALL OVER EUROPE LATELY...AS AMBASSADORS FOR SWEDISH POP!

THAT'S RIGHT! NOW EVERYONE RESPECTS SWEDISH MUSIC! IF IT HADN'T BEEN FOR ABBA...

OUR PEOPLE KNEW WE'D DONE THE RIGHT THING, TO FOLLOW UP OUR SUCCESS OUTSIDE OUR OWN COUNTRY. AND NOW..?

AND NOW! JUST THE CONTINUED DEDICATION OF PRODUCING THE RIGHT SONGS FOR YOU. AND TO STAY THERE AT THE TOP OF THEIR PROFESSION...WHERE YOU AND YOUR SUPPORT KEEP THEM!

WATERLOO—I WAS DEFEATED, YOU WON THE WAR, WATERLOO—PROMISE TO LOVE YOU FOR EVERMORE...

14th January 1978

More from our Swedish superstars next week!

SNAKE . LISTEN, LADY—I'M A POOR MAN, BUT I GOTTA REWARD YOU...

NO WAY! I WOULDN'T *THINK* OF...

THE MAN, CLEARLY ECCENTRIC WILL SAY NO MORE. JAIME GETS HIS HORSES BACK FOR HIM... CALMS THEM.

TAKE THIS. I INSIST. IT WAS BEQUEATHED TO ME BY MY GREAT UNCLE EBENEEZER. I DON'T KNOW WHAT THE KEY WILL BRING— BUT IT'S YOURS WHEN YOU GO TO THE *HOUSE OF THE SIX LOCKS!*

THANK YOU ONCE AGAIN. REMEMBER— THE HOUSE OF THE SIX LOCKS. FOLKS ROUND HERE KNOW IT...

JAIME THINKS LITTLE MORE ABOUT IT, UNTIL THAT EVENING. IN THE COUNTRY HOTEL WHERE SHE'S STAYING...

WELL, OLD EBENEEZER KANE'S DEAD AT LAST.

THAT'LL MEAN HIS KIN WILL BE ROLLIN' UP AT THE HOUSE OF THE SIX LOCKS. WE'LL BE HEARIN' ABOUT THE MYSTERY OF THE OLD VAULT...

EXCUSE ME—COULDN'T HELP OVERHEARING. WHAT'S THE STORY ABOUT THIS HOUSE..?

HEYYY! YOU GOT ONE O' THE KEYS! BUT YOU AIN'T KIN OF EBENEEZER, OR YOU'D KNOW...

JAIME SITS DOWN AND EXPLAINS, AND THEN A STRANGE TALE IS UNFOLDED!

THERE'S SOME SECRET LOCKED AWAY BENEATH THE HOUSE. MAYBE A FORTUNE! FOLK SAY THERE'S A HUGE DOOR, WITH SIX LOCKS...

EACH OF SIX SURVIVIN' RELATIVES HAS A KEY. EBENEEZER WAS A WEIRD AN' LONELY GUY... I FIGURE THERE'S *DEMONS* IN THAT VAULT, WAITIN'!... TO BE RELEASED!

INTRIGUED, JAIME DECIDES TO FOLLOW IT UP...

BESIDES... IF I DON'T TURN UP WITH THIS, THE VAULT WON'T BE OPENED AT ALL! THIS COULD BE *FUN*...

BUT HER FIRST GLIMPSE OF THE HOUSE OF THE SIX LOCKS, SET DEEP IN A REMOTE FOREST, IS FAR FROM REASSURING!

JUPITER! WHAT A SPOOKY PLACE! IF I BELIEVED IN SUCH THINGS, I COULD ALMOST SENSE AN *EVIL* ATMOSPHERE...

24th June 1978

It used to be called Punk Rock. Now it's the New Wave, and it's a million miles away from the Abba Sound, The Bay City Rollers and David Soul. Whatever you think about it, (and we'd love to know★), it's hit the music scene in a big way recently — The Ramones got there first with their "Sheena's A Punk Rocker", while the Stranglers have done nicely, thankyou, on the beaches with "Peaches". So here's our special look — containing an exclusive interview with Barrie Masters of Eddie And The Hot Rods — at the music that some people claim is the sound of the seventies, and others sum up in just one word — Rubbish!

THE NEW WAVE
What's Happening?

Well, what is your view of the New Wave? It's certainly caught on with the zeal and enthusiasm that helped the sixties pop music boom take off. You probably won't recall that period when the mods took to their scooters, and The Who became heroes for thousands of city kids.

The Who, in a way, were the sixties equivalent of today's new wave bands. Pete Townshend would thrash around on lead guitar, while Keith Moon hardly showed much interest in the well-being of his drum-kit! The band were — and still are — loud and raucous. Commercially they were a great success, whereas the 'godfather' of punk rock — Lou Reed — remained an underground cult figure in the late sixties with his weird band of musicians, The Velvet Underground.

Along came the Seventies — Glitter rock, David Cassidy and The Osmonds. The raw power of the sixties beat boom had gone, and was sadly missed by many. Something exciting and 'back to the roots' was wanted. It came alright, in an explosion of electric energy, with the New Wave groups just over a year ago — and their screaming brand of rock 'n 'roll.

The Ramones arrived from America, Dr. Feelgood made us feel just that from Canvey Island, and Eddie And The Hot Rods bounced in and out of the lower reaches of the chart. All roared like lions, and played

(Above) The Who in '65 — the earliest punk band?
(Below) Lou Reed today — New Wave's Godfather.

guitars like lightning.

The cat was out of the bag, and new wave groups flourished. The Damned, The Clash, The Stranglers and The Jam — who many see as the 'new Who' — all appeared from the London Underworld, and punk followers moved to their new shrine, the Roxy Club in London's Covent Garden.

"I suppose we were the first 'new wave' type band," Eddie And The Hot Rods' energetic lead singer Barrie Masters told Richard Tippett. *"We never tried to start anything, though. We came along at the same time as Dr. Feelgood, but never went out of our way to be new wave or anything. It's mainly because we came on to the scene at about the same time — or just before — the punk thing started.*

"We really don't like being called a 'new wave' band. It's a contradictory name. People take it in different ways. New wave, yeah, because we're a new band. But beyond that, we don't consider ourselves in the same category as the normal punk bands."

The name Eddie And The Hot Rods is a good 'un. Where did it come from? *"We were just driving along one day, and someone turned around and said it. In those days, just after the heavy metal era, it seemed a bit outrageous to be called something like that. So we stuck with it. Good for our type of rock 'n'roll."*

OK, so Barrie doesn't see the band as punk rockers. Then what? *"Well, music wise,*

The Damned   The Stranglers

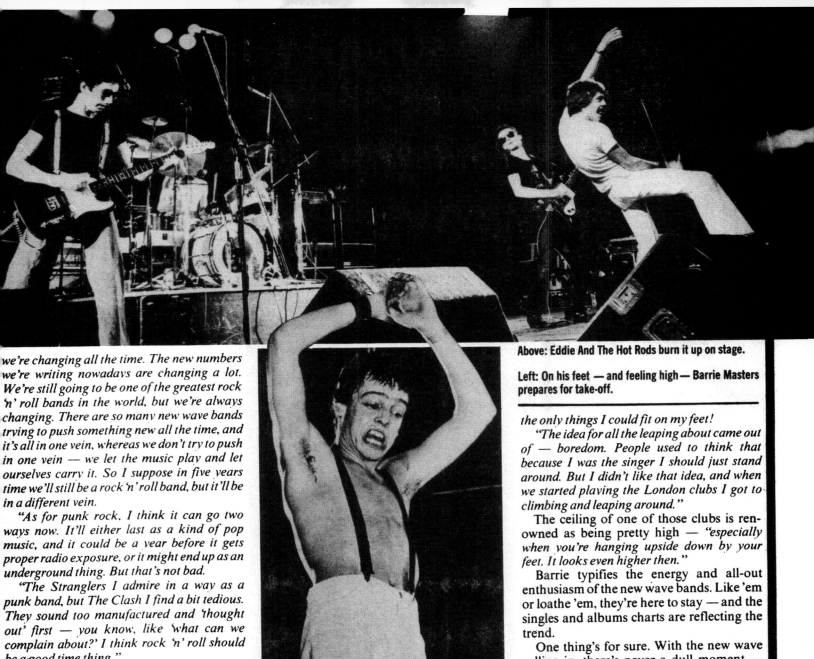

we're changing all the time. The new numbers we're writing nowadays are changing a lot. We're still going to be one of the greatest rock 'n' roll bands in the world, but we're always changing. There are so many new wave bands trying to push something new all the time, and it's all in one vein, whereas we don't try to push in one vein — we let the music play and let ourselves carry it. So I suppose in five years time we'll still be a rock 'n' roll band, but it'll be in a different vein.

"As for punk rock, I think it can go two ways now. It'll either last as a kind of pop music, and it could be a year before it gets proper radio exposure, or it might end up as an underground thing. But that's not bad.

"The Stranglers I admire in a way as a punk band, but The Clash I find a bit tedious. They sound too manufactured and 'thought out' first — you know, like 'what can we complain about?' I think rock 'n' roll should be a good time thing."

Anyone who's seen Eddie And The Hot Rods will know all about Barrie's belief in a good time. When he's on stage, anything can happen (and usually does) from climbing beams to leaping about like a circus acrobat. "I've had my problems, though," said Barrie. "I fell off the stage once. I did a really beautiful flying somersault and the stage ran out! I landed on the stairs, and couldn't walk after it. I had to wear a pair of heavy Dr. Martins boots for a week on stage after that, 'cos they were

Above: Eddie And The Hot Rods burn it up on stage.

Left: On his feet — and feeling high — Barrie Masters prepares for take-off.

the only things I could fit on my feet!

"The idea for all the leaping about came out of — boredom. People used to think that because I was the singer I should just stand around. But I didn't like that idea, and when we started playing the London clubs I got to climbing and leaping around."

The ceiling of one of those clubs is renowned as being pretty high — "especially when you're hanging upside down by your feet. It looks even higher then."

Barrie typifies the energy and all-out enthusiasm of the new wave bands. Like 'em or loathe 'em, they're here to stay — and the singles and albums charts are reflecting the trend.

One thing's for sure. With the new wave rolling in, there's never a dull moment — whether you think it's Punk or Junk.

★ **What do you think of the New Wave? Rubbish or Sound Of The Seventies? We'll print the most interesting of your letters on the subject. Write to: New Wave Debate. Look-in, 247, Tottenham Court Road, London, W1P 0AU. And don't forget to include your age when you write.**

The Clash

The Jam

LENA LOOKS AHEAD

WHEN LENA ZAVARONI rocketed to fame with her recording of 'Ma He's Making Eyes At Me' back in January 1974, (it reached the number eight slot in the British charts), she was the youngest-ever artist to appear on 'Top Of The Pops'. Now just three short years later, little Lena is one of the hottest properties in showbusiness and a half-millionairess.

★ Recently Look-in's Peter Jeffries spoke to Lena during her rehearsals and asked: "Are you glad you started your career at such an early age or would you have preferred a more natural childhood?" "Well, I'm quite glad really," she explained, "especially now, because I'm at stage school which means I'm not treated any differently from the other kids."

Does she find it difficult to fit her studies in with rehearsals? "Sometimes," she answered, "but we usually manage it some way or another. It very rarely comes to the point where I miss out on anything. Any spare time I do get I'm usually found in front of the TV — in fact I think I'm in danger of developing square eyes. My main hobby, though, is horse-riding. I had my own pony at one time but it wasn't fair to keep it in London so we found it a nice home in the country."

Lena's worked with many world-famous stars in her relatively short career but which of them has impressed her the most? "Oh, I couldn't really say. All of them were equally nice. Bruce Forsyth was lovely and I really enjoyed working with Leslie Crowther; he really is funny. When I first went to America I appeared in a charity show in Hollywood with Frank Sinatra and Lucille Ball, and after the show, Lucille said to me: 'You're special, very special, and very, very good', which was a really nice compliment from such a talented person whom I admire tremendously."

Lena has come a long way since those kind words from Lucille Ball, in fact she has not only lived up to that praise but has shown that she can go right to the top of the showbiz world. And so to 1977 which presents yet another challenge to Britain's youngest superstar and sees the release of a brand new single on the Galaxy label, 'Air Love', and an album, 'Presenting Lena Zavaroni'. As her great friend Hughie Green would say: 'The sky's the limit for Lena'.

30th July 1977

WHAT A TEAM!
YOU AND THE SIX MILLION DOLLAR MAN

Just think of all the adventure-packed missions you could undertake with this terrific all-action figure of Colonel Steve Austin.

And like Steve himself, he's bionic all the way through. Roll back his skin to reveal removable bionic modules. Or activate a secret button in his back and he'll lift an engine block with one hand.

You can even re-create bionic vision by looking through his bionic eye!

Steve, and all the fantastic games and accessories below, are waiting for you at your toy shop. So start on your first bionic mission right now, and get down there as fast as you can.

Bionic Vision
A wide angle lens allows you to see through his eye, and create bionic vision for yourself.

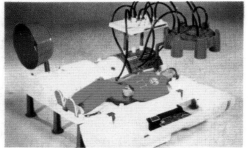

Bionic Transporter and Repair Station
Closed up, it's a Bionic Transporter with rocket-like features to whisk Steve to assignments in outer space. Open the back and you have a re-vitalisation chamber. Flip the front open and it's an operating theatre for bionic surgery.

Adventure Sets
Three terrific outfits for you to collect. An astronaut suit. A jet pilot's flying suit. And a smart blue denim casual suit. Plus portable bionic system.

Bionic Board Games
The Six Million Dollar Man, Bionic Woman, and Bionic Crisis, three fantastic games for all the family to play.

Bionic Arm
You operate a secret button in Steve's back and he'll lift an engine block with one hand!

Back-Pack Radio and Helmet
Listen-in to Steve Austin's secret assignment messages with this super crystal radio that actually works without batteries or electricity.

THE SIX MILLION DOLLAR MAN
T.M. ©1976

BY DENYS FISHER

DENYS FISHER TOYS, Retail Sales Division, Thorp Arch Trading Estate, Wetherby LS23 7BL, England.

THE BIONIC WOMAN™

A MAN SHE RESCUES FROM DEATH GIVES JAIME SOMMERS A KEY-ONE OF A SET NEEDED TO OPEN THE MYSTERIOUS VAULT BENEATH THE LONELY MANSION KNOWN AS THE HOUSE OF THE SIX LOCKS. INTRIGUED, JAIME FINDS THE PLACE...AND IS ALMOST PHYSICALLY REPELLED BY THE EVIL, BROODING ATMOSPHERE

UGGH! IT GIVES ME THE SHIVERS! BUT THERE'S NO SENSE IN GOING BACK NOW!

AS IF IN ANSWER TO THE GROAN OF THE RUSTED IRON, THE MAIN DOOR OF THE HOUSE CREAKS OPEN...

YOU ARE NO KIN OF THE LATE EBENEEZER KANE! WHAT IS YOUR BUSINESS HERE?

I-I WAS GIVEN A KEY...

WHOEVER HOLDS THE KEYS HAS THE RIGHT! ENTER!

WAIT. I WILL ANNOUNCE YOU!

ER-MY NAME'S JAIME SOMMERS...

CHEEE! WHAT HAVE I WALKED INTO..?

JAIME'S NERVES ARE HARDLY CALMED WHEN SHE'S USHERED INTO THE DRAWING ROOM...

COME IN, MISS SOMMERS, COME IN! MY NAME IS KELMAN BREECH. I AM THE FAMILY LAWYER!

I BID YOU-ER-WELCOME. AS-ER-ER-SPOKESMAN. YES, SPOKESMAN. I AM BEAUREGARD KANE, MA'AM...

ALLOW ME TO INTRODUCE-ER- COUSIN CLAYMAN KANE. MISS SARAH KANE...

I'M AFRAID I REALLY SHOULDN'T BE HERE...

1st July 1978

1st July 1978

Is this the end for Jaime? More on page 114

STEWPOT'S NEWSDESK

RELIC RUMMAGE

There's a programme running at present called 'Elusive Butterflies' from Southern TV, presented by Gordon Trebilcock, which so fascinated me that I visited him at his home in mid-Wiltshire. After a butterfly-spotting-safari, he let me into a secret. He is working on an idea for another fascinating show which will teach people to use their eyes when walking around towns and villages. "Our country is packed with exciting stories going back centuries," he said. And there are many instances of young people playing history-detective and finding important historic data. For instance, in his own village, one of his young sons pointed out some odd square holes high up on an old wall. They turned out to be supports for beams, probably moved from a large unknown castle nearby. So the hunt proceeded for a local fortress, and a bottomless wealth of stories.

Do you think there's anything like that near you? Your local historical society may give you a start to becoming a history-detective — a great holiday activity! Let me know at Look-in if you unearth any ancient excitement. A reporter's certificate to senders of entries used.

WHAT A SCREAM!

★★★★★★★★★★★★★★★★★★★★★★★★

A while ago, Pauline Quirke asked on her TV show Pauline's Quirkes: "why do girls scream at pop stars"? She had a few replies, but hardly as many as I received when I asked the same question on these pages.

It seems you all have your own theories as to why the young ladies of Britain have to regularly reach for the throat spray! The best letters, printed here, earn their senders tickets for a TV show. If you're a winner, congratulations — if not, please don't shout and scream about it . . .

★★★★★★★★★★★★★★★★★★★★★★★★

Everyone has a lot of emotions locked inside them. Sometimes the emotions have to be let loose. Well, at a concert it's a great place because the excitement of going to see your favourite group triggers off all the other emotions and by having a good scream you can get it all out of you.

When you're at school, you can't scream to get rid of your feelings so it often ends up that you argue with someone or even get into a fight. Because you can't scream every day it makes you want to take the chance to have a good yell when you can.
Sue (no surname supplied), Benfleet, Essex.

I'll tell you why we nutters scream at shows. I went to the last two programmes of **Pauline's Quirkes** and it's true that we scream partly to raise attention, but that's not the only reason! It's the only time you have to let off steam (so to speak!) and if you shout loud you may find yourself listening to your remarks on the show! But I've also found that if you go with a friend and you're sitting there calling Derek, she'll suddenly scream **Bill,** and drown you. Well, you're not going to stand for that, are you? Definitely not! So — obvious thing to do, you scream **DEREK** ten times louder than her. So her Bill is drowned by your Derek. But then she gets her own back — twenty times louder. And you both end up not being able to even whisper your favourite's name the next day.
Janet Ruff, Thornton Heath, Surrey.

My twin sister and I scream at Flintlock concerts because we think that our tonsils will give up on us and then we will have to go to hospital — where we hope Flintlock will come and visit us!
Carol and Maria Sanders, London, E.2.

27th August 1977

Because there are various departments in Look-in, it is necessary to have different addresses for your letters, competitions, etc. If this were not so, it would be very difficult to process the many reports and entries the editor receives from readers. As you know, the competitions in Look-in should be sent to P.O. Box 141, London SE6 3HR. That address is for competition entries only and no other letters or reports should be sent there.

All other letters, unless otherwise stated, should be sent to Look-in, 247 Tottenham Court Road, London W1P 0AU.

Whilst on the subject of letters, please DO NOT ask us to send you information or photographs. It has always been Look-in's policy not to issue photographs, for in most cases the pictures do not belong to us, but to the photographers themselves.

SKATEBOARDING CORRECTION

I have never been to a concert and I think that the people at one should be allowed to scream, but only before and after the group has finished playing. If they scream during the concert they spoil it for other people (who only go to listen) because they can't hear. Also the group playing might as well just go up on stage and stand there doing nothing and the people can scream their heads off. But if the group is playing, then anyone screaming should be taken out or the concert stopped.
Debbie Tite, Bolton.

I think you were right when you said that some girls scream because they hope to get a private smile of their own; another reason, I think, is the one Tony Prince gave on the 4th Pauline Quirke show — that when you've been waiting weeks to see your fave group, you're really nervous, excited and tense before the concert, and when, suddenly, you see your idols for the first time in the flesh, you just let off all your pent-up emotions in screams. I also think that screaming is very infectious. If everyone else except you was screaming you'd feel very strange, so you'd start — their excitement would be infectious, too, and so you'd soon probably be screaming for yourself, not just because everyone else was. I know that if nobody else was screaming, I and most other fans wouldn't have the courage to start screaming on our own, but since the bulk of fans **do**, then everyone else joins in.

One point to finish with — if a group like Flintlock went on stage in front of hundreds of girls, I think they'd think something was **very** wrong if all the girls were staring at them poker-faced and no-one was screaming — wouldn't they?
Rosie Dewar, Midlothian.

When all year round you have listened to Flintlock records as much as you can, you have posters of them all over your wall, you daydream of them whenever you can, you think of them when you go to sleep, you dream of them at night and you drive everybody mad with the word 'Flintlock' . . . then, when you have been through all that and you get that close to them, that's enough to make anybody scream blue murder, isn't it?
Barbara Ingram, High Wycombe, Bucks.

We have received a fair share of letters from readers who wrote away for more information about skateboarding addressing their letters to the address that was included in Look-in as part of a feature on the sport.

Unfortunately, the address we printed was incorrect, and the editor apologises for any concern that may have been caused by the error.

But fear not, skateboarders of Britain. Stewpot has put everything to rights, and now I can give you the correct address for your letters should you wish to learn more about skateboarding. So, pens at the ready, here it is: **Barry Walsh, British Safety Council, 62, Chancellors Road, London, W.6.**

IT'S MARC!

Don't forget to watch the new series that begins this Wednesday (the 24th) at 4.20. Entitled Marc, it features the talents of Marc Bolan in the first of a six-week series that will showcase the talents of some of our top artists.

Marc's group, T.Rex, are involved in the action every week, and also on the first show are Showaddywaddy, Stephanie de Sykes and The Jam.

It's enough to make you scream aloud, isn't it . . ?—Ed.

A super success ...that's the Look-in Star Awards

Magpie on Tuesday was the place to be for Look-in fans. 'Cos on that day, it was **your** vote that really counted (to quote a well-known TV celebrity!) The Look-in Star Awards were the highlight of the highly popular Thames TV show, and for the first time you were able to find out just who you voted as winners in our recent Star Poll. Remember, there are more than two million of you out there who read Look-in. And it was from your votes the top ITV personalities were chosen.

It's an upside-down world for Richard O'Sullivan in Australia — but back home things certainly looked the right way up for him.

Joanna Lumley — your favourite female personality.

The winners? Well, to recap for you, Richard O'Sullivan and Joanna Lumley took the main Awards as top TV personalities. Richard has been in Australia for sometime, however, and so we are unable to picture him.

★ ★

The other Awards covered a wide spectrum —
here they are for you:

Stewpot meets the New Avengers and presents their Star Award to producer Brian Clemens (left)

The Ghosts from Motley Hall get together with producer Quentin Lawrence

TOP FAMILY PROGRAMME:
The New Avengers (Thames)

Right: Runaround's Stan Boardman shares a joke — and an Award — with Stewpot.

TOP TV SPORTS STAR:
Kevin Keegan

TOP COMEDY PROGRAMME:
The Ghosts Of Motley Hall
(Granada Television)

TOP GENERAL/MAGAZINE
PROGRAMME:
Magpie (Thames Television)

Kevin Keegan — Fave footballer of '77.

TOP MUSIC/LIGHT ENTERTAINMENT PROGRAMME:
Runaround (Southern Television)

TOP DRAMA PROGRAMME:
The Tomorrow People (Thames Television)

Mike Holoway accepts the Drama Award — with Tomorrow People producer Roger Price

Magpie's Mick Robertson — this magazine show reigns supreme.

TOP TV POP STARS:
Showaddywaddy

SPECIAL AWARD: TOP RECORD:
Under The Moon Of Love **by Showaddywaddy**

Congratulations to all concerned on your Awards. And many thanks also to the thousands of you Look-in readers who made our very first Star Awards so successful. Here's to next year . . .

113

Murder at the manor!

THE BIONIC WOMAN™

GIVEN A KEY BY A MAN SHE RESCUES, JAIME SOMMERS FINDS HERSELF IN THE STRANGE AND SINISTER HOUSE OF THE SIX LOCKS, WHERE FIVE OTHER KEY-HOLDERS, RELATIVES OF THE DECEASED RECLUSE EBENEEZER KANE, ARE WAITING TO OPEN THE SECRET VAULT TO DISCOVER ITS MYSTERIES! AS THE GAUNT BUTLER DIRECTS HER TO HER ROOM, JAIME HEARS THE WARNING YELL FROM KELMAN BREECH, THE FAMILY LAWYER...

MISS SOMMERS! **LOOK OUT!**

GOOD GRIEF!

WITH ALL THE STRENGTH OF HER BIONIC MUSCLES, JAIME FLINGS HERSELF BACKWARDS!

MY DEAR GIRL! ARE YOU ALL RIGHT..?

WHEW! IF THAT THING HAD **HIT** ME...

WHAT'S GOING ON?

A NEAR CALAMITY! A DREADFUL ACCIDENT! THANK GOODNESS I SAW IT!

YOU SAVED MY LIFE, MR. BREECH...

YOU'D BETTER CLEAN UP THE MESS, KRAKE. I'LL SHOW MISS SOMMERS UPSTAIRS.

AS YOU SAY, SIR.

ALONE IN HER ROOM, JAIME STRUGGLES TO CONTROL HER JUMPING NERVES...

WHATEVER MADE ME COME HERE? I DON'T BELONG! I FEEL LIKE EVERYTHING- EVEN THE HOUSE ITSELF- **RESENTS ME!**

Who is the killer? More on page 118

TOMORROW'S PERSON

An exclusive interview with Nicholas Young

WHEN Robin Tucek spoke to Nicholas Young recently, he had just heard that 'The Tomorrow People' had been voted top drama programme in the Look-in Star awards . . .

Nick, who plays senior Tomorrow Person John, was naturally thrilled with the programme's success and was looking forward to starting work on a new series of six episodes. We talked first about his 60 appearances as a Tomorrow Person but, as Nick pointed out, he and John are *not* both the same person and Nick does enjoy his other roles, especially the comedy ones!

"*We are hoping to start work on the new* **Tomorrow People** *series soon, but first a date has to be sorted out to suit everyone involved. Obviously it is a problem, as studio time is hard to come by and everything has to be carefully planned.*"

There has been another personnel change in the cast.

"*Yes, in fact, I'm the only one left from the original cast. Elizabeth Adare is being re-*

placed in the new series, but that's only because she has just had a baby! She might well return. The new girl is Misako Koba who is Japanese."

Obviously, being a Tomorrow Person is very important to Nick, but first and foremost he is an actor. What plans has he in mind career wise?

'I have had an invitation, believe it or not, to direct a film'

"*I'm getting to the stage where I'd like to do something other than* **The Tomorrow People***. Obviously I do other things such as TV commercials. One that I did that was great fun was when I played Robin of 'Batman and Robin' at Christmas for a battery commercial. I did a record with Batman called 'Batman & Robin' which died a death — you might have read about it in Look-in! At the moment my time is being taken up appearing in a comedy film. I think that people tend to take me far too seriously, I'm very rarely allowed to do much comedy.*

"*In fact one of the things I enjoyed most of all was a play I did at Canterbury a couple of*

years ago in which I played a pop star. It was a comedy, in which I had to play the guitar as well. I've been playing the electric guitar since I was seventeen and it's not something I've ever been able to do professionally apart from that particular play. I'd certainly like to play the guitar professionally if it were possible.

"*I've also been involved in the production of a couple of things. One is a motor racing film, as yet untitled, which some friends of mine put*

Nick with Elizabeth Adare

up the money for — and we're going to be producing that in France this summer. I've been down to Cannes two or three times already this year, helping on the production side and getting things set up, but it doesn't look as if it's going to be made until the spring.

"*Apart from that I have had an invitation, believe it or not, to direct a film. It's very early days yet and at the moment it's a question of getting the finance. It would be a domestic British film intended primarily for the British market so it's not a big budget affair. That's something I may be doing this summer, provided we get the money and time.*

"*I seem to be working on all aspects of the business. When I'm not actually working as an actor, I very often help my agent out. In fact, when they were casting for* **The Tomorrow People** *I was working in my agent's office and the producer rang up and asked for our suggestions for actors for the series. As I was there, I got the job of putting all the photographs in the envelopes and sending them off to Thames — and I included my own . . . !*

"*I really would like to do more comedy, although I love working on* **The Tomorrow People***. I'd like to do something completely different on TV because at the moment I'm very much associated with* **The Tomorrow People***. If anybody sees me in the street they always say — oh, it's John of* **Tomorrow's World** *. . . as they always call it. You get so totally identified with John that it's not terribly good for you as an actor . . . they just can't see you as anybody else.*"

★ **Keep you eyes open for brand new adventures of The Tomorrow People on screen in a few months' time.**

Colour pin-up: Bert Hill 20th August 1977

117

THE BIONIC WOMAN™

GIVEN A KEY — ONE OF SIX REQUIRED TO OPEN THE MYSTERIOUS VAULT IN THE HOUSE OF THE SIX LOCKS, THE GRIM AND LONELY MANSION OF THE RECLUSE EBENEEZER KANE, DECEASED, JAIME SOMMERS FINDS HERSELF PLUNGED INTO SINISTER DANGER! AN ATTEMPT ON HER LIFE FAILS, BUT ONE OF THE FIVE KANE RELATIVES PRESENT, CLAYMAN KANE, IS STABBED TO DEATH!

ONE OF THE OTHERS HAS TO BE THE KILLER! BUT WHICH...? OR MAYBE KRAKE, THE BUTLER...EVEN THOUGH HE WARNED ME TO BE ON MY GUARD!

SURELY NOT MR. BREECH, THEIR LAWYER. IT WAS HIM WHO SAVED MY LIFE...

MY BELIEF, MISS SOMMERS, IS THAT THE GHOST OF EBENEEZER KANE COMMITS THIS EVIL!

OHHH!

WHAT AN AWFUL SHOCK YOU GAVE ME! JABEZ... ISN'T IT?

THAT IS MY NAME. I DABBLE IN THE OCCULT. I HAVE A FEELING FOR THE WORLD BEYOND. THERE IS...

OH, NNNO!

SUDDENLY, THE SENTENCE CHOKES OFF! HIS FACE TWISTED, JABEZ KANE LURCHES FORWARD!

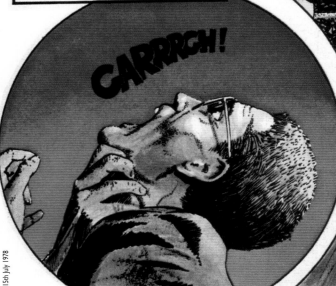

GARRRGH!

JAIME'S CRY ROUSES THE HOUSEHOLD AGAIN!

POISION, I SHOULD SAY.

HE ALWAYS HAD A FLASK OF WATER BY HIS BEDSIDE.

DASHED UNHEALTHY. PREFER-ER-SOMETHING-ER STRONGER... MYSELF.

HE WAS AN UNDERTAKER. WONDER IF HE BROUGHT A COFFIN WITH HIM..?

THAT, MERRYMAN IS IN VERY BAD TASTE!

UHHH... YEAH.

LISTEN, EVERYONE! THIS IS IMPORTANT! THERE ARE SIX OF US HERE, AND FIVE ARE IN DEADLY DANGER...

ONE OF US IS A MURDERER. WE MUST KEEP TOGETHER FROM NOW ON. WATCH EACH OTHER.

IT'S AGREED ON. BUT FIRST KRAKE HAS TO REMOVE THE BODY... AND SARAH AND BEAUREGARD KANE BOTH WANT THINGS FROM THEIR ROOMS...

YOU'RE A CALM WOMAN, MISS SOMMERS. WHAT DO YOU SUGGEST..?

TO PASS THE TIME? CARDS-ANYTHING!

ME, I COULD DO WITH A SNORT OUT OF BEAUREGARD'S BOTTLE WHEN HE BRINGS IT DOWN!

BUT BEAUREGARD'S DRINKING DAYS ARE ARE OVER! A YELL OF FEAR, A SPLINTERING CRASH, AND...

KA RASSH

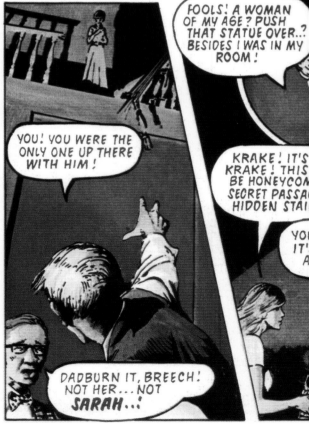

FOOLS! A WOMAN OF MY AGE? PUSH THAT STATUE OVER..? BESIDES I WAS IN MY ROOM!

YOU! YOU WERE THE ONLY ONE UP THERE WITH HIM!

KRAKE! IT'S GOT TO BE KRAKE! THIS PLACE MUST BE HONEYCOMBED WITH SECRET PASSAGES AND HIDDEN STAIRWAYS...

YOU'RE RIGHT! IT'S THE ONLY ANSWER!

DADBURN IT, BREECH! NOT HER... NOT SARAH...!

BUT HORROR PILES ON HORROR! WITH A SHRIEK OF RENDING WOOD, BOARDS AT THE HEAD OF THE STAIRS GIVE WAY!

AIEEEE!

SKRUNNCH

Continued on page 122

15th July 1978

Another of our looks at your local ITV shows. This time it's plenty of custard pies — the recipe of success for . . .

TISWAS!

IF you're visiting the *Tiswas* studios in Birmingham for the Saturday morning spectacular that gives new meaning to three hours well spent, then don't think you're going to have an easy time of it. The peaceable person looking for a quiet life had better not expect a comfortable ride in the protection of the TV studio audience. Chris Tarrant, Sally James and Trevor East will see to it that all hell breaks loose — so armour plating rather than T-shirts are the order of the day for the show.

When Look-in's **Richard Tippett** went to ATV to interview Chris and Sally after another hectic performance, in which they probably lost as many pounds in weight as they gained in their pay packets, the atmosphere of chaos still lingered — the interview took place in the studio canteen amid clashing cutlery and chinking tea cups and saucers!

Nevertheless, Christopher and Sal — as they tend to call each other — were as bubbly and alive as ever. Oh, and John Conteh hadn't turned up as the main guest on the show, but never mind. Said Chris: "To be fair, John is usually a very reliable bloke; it's the first time this has ever happened in nearly 200 shows. We've had guests who've been late, but it's the first time a guest actually hasn't appeared at all."

So how did the quick-thinking madcaps re-arrange the format, remembering that it's all live? "We literally re-wrote the last half-hour of the show in ten minutes," answered Chris. "Re-jigged it at ten to twelve while on the air. But we'd a lot of contingency plans in case John Conteh did arrive late."

Continued Sally: "We've always got sack loads of mail we can go through; there are a million and a half things we can do. Today, for instance, we quickly put in a routine getting the kids to do tongue-twisters. Somebody rushed up to 'graphics', got hold of some tongue-twisting graphics, and Chris did a little spot."

Chris spoke about the enjoyable mayhem that's part and parcel of *Tiswas*. "We've been doing the tongue-twisting thing for about four years. We get a big pile of LPs and a lot of custard pies, and you get some kids as volunteers — they all volunteer — and you say: 'Here's a tongue-twister — the sinking steamer slowly sank, or whatever. If you can read that out as quickly as possible, twice, you will get five of these LPs. If you don't, you will be struck by a mystery object.' Literally, in four years, I have never given away a single LP . . ."

Chris and Sally have some very solid and immovable opinions about their studio audience. "They don't like it if you don't smack them with a custard pie," they said in unison.

"At the studio before the show, they're all bubbling over with energy," said Sally. "They know the programme so well. They go away unhappy if they don't get a custard pie." Chipped in Chris: "They get up at about six o'clock in the morning with excitement."

For those who've never seen *Tiswas* — and it's becoming more and more popular in various ITV

regions other than ATV — Chris gave a brief history of the programme. Or, in particular, the show's name itself. "It originally was called *Today Is Saturday*, and it was a bit of a shambles. Very live, very rough and ready television. We used the initials of the show (TIS) and the WAS (*Watch And See*) just cottoned on to the end. Because *Today Is Saturday* was such a naff title, we decided to stick with *Tiswas*."

There's never a dull moment on *Tiswas* as Trevor (dark hair) Chris (blond) and Sally make very sure. (Right) a typical example of mayhem — we won't attempt to sort out who's who, or even what's happening!

8th April 1978

Laugh along with another of Benny's relations next week.

THE BIONIC WOMAN

YEEAARRGH!

GIVEN A KEY — ONE OF SIX REQUIRED TO OPEN THE MYSTERIOUS VAULT IN THE GRIM AND LONELY HOUSE OF THE SIX LOCKS, ONCE OWNED BY RECLUSE EBENEEZER KANE, NOW DECEASED, JAIME SOMMERS FINDS HERSELF IN A NIGHTMARE! THREE OF THE KANES ARE MURDERED, AND NOW A FOURTH DIES AS A STAIRCASE COLLAPSES.

JAIME LEADS THE RUSH...

THESE BOARDS HAVE BEEN WEAKENED! LOOK — THERE'S SOME KIND OF RELEASE GADGET!

KELMAN BREECH, THE FAMILY LAWYER CLUTCHES HER SLEEVE...

COME DOWN! WE **MUST** THINK IN TERMS OF SELF-PRESERVATION! WE'RE THE ONLY ONES LEFT... YOU, ME AND MERRYMAN KANE!

EXCEPT FOR KRAKE THE BUTLER! WHERE'S HE VANISHED TO? **HE'S** GOT TO BE BEHIND ALL THIS!

THERE IS NO SIGN OF THE SINISTER RETAINER. HE SEEMS TO HAVE UTTERLY DISAPPEARED!

WHEN'S IT GONNA BE MORNING? ALL I WANNA DO IS OPEN THAT VAULT AND THEN GET THE BLAZES **OUTTA** HERE!

WAIT A MINUTE! THE KEYS! I HAVE MINE — YOU HAVE YOURS...

IF KRAKE'S TAKEN THE OTHERS OFF HIS VICTIMS HE'LL BE GETTING SARAH'S RIGHT **NOW**..!

NO, MISS SOMMERS YOU **CAN'T** GO DOWN THERE!

SOMEONE'S GOT TO STOP THIS SLAUGHTER, MERRY-MAN! BELIEVE ME — I CAN DO IT!

22nd July 1978

THE DROP THAT KILLED SARAH IS NOTHING TO THE BIONIC WOMAN!

NO KEY. I'M GONNA FIND WHERE THOSE STAIRS LEAD... AND IF KRAKE TRIES TO STOP ME...

THE DANK STENCH, THE BRUSHING COBWEBS AND THE FLICKERING SHADOWS ARE ENOUGH TO TAX THE STRONGEST NERVES...

UUUGGH! I CAN ALMOST FEEL THE EVIL DOWN HERE!

SUDDENLY...

KLEKK!

MERRYMAN!

MISS- MISS SOMMERS! I- I...

AAARGH!

SHOCKED BY MERRYMAN'S DEATH, JAIME DOESN'T NOTICE THE MENACING SHADOW LOOM UP BEHIND HER!

A HAPPY YULETIDE HOLIDAY ON ITV

There's a bumper bundle of programmes coming your way this Christmas week on ITV that's guaranteed to make your holiday sparkle with fun and thrills. Amongst the stars who will be brightening up your screens are Morecambe and Wise, Kermit, Danny Kaye, Charlie's lovely Angels, Benny Hill, Yootha Joyce, Brian Murphy and a host of others. So here's a brief run-down on the fabulous entertainment you'll not want to miss.

Saturday 23rd Dec.

6.45 Celebrity Squares Special

Bob Monkhouse introduces an all-star line-up for this special Christmas edition of the big box game. In the firing line of questions will be John Conteh, Gemma Craven, Leslie Crowther, Sacha Distel, Dick Emery, Noele Gordon, Frankie Howerd, Elaine Strich and, of course, regular 'boxer' Willie Rushton. They'll be helping one of the contestants to win a trip to Disneyland or £1,000.

★●★●★●★●★●★●★○

Sunday 24th Dec.

7.15 Bruce Forsyth's Christmas Eve

Bruce will be hosting this fun-packed two-hour show with the aid, of course, of the lovely Anthea Redfern. There will be lots of guest stars, competitions with big prizes and regular inserts The Glums and The Worker.

Nice to see you —
Bruce Forsyth.

Monday 25th Dec.

9.00 a.m. The Wotsit From Whizz-Bang

Christmas Day kicks off with this delightful story read by Joe Lynch. The Wotsit, Thingummy and Oojah live in Whizz-Bang, which is somewhere between almost nowhere and not quite anywhere and where the time is always half-past four. One day a boy called Andy is playing in the garden when the Wotsit whizz-bangs into the cabbage patch and starts off this great series.

●★●★●★●★●★●★●★

9.25 Christmas Clapperboard

In this programme Chris Kelly looks at films about flying without planes. He'll be showing you clips from **Superman, Dumbo, The Cat From Outer Space, The Thief Of Baghdad, Herbie, The Absent-Minded Professor** and **Chitty Chitty Bang Bang.**

●★●★●★●★●★●★●★

2.00 3-2-1 Special

Supported by his lovely secretaries and regular team of jokers Jack Douglas, Duggie Brown and Chris Emmet, Ted Rogers will be conducting this special 1,000 to One quiz. Three celebrity couples will be trying to win £3,000 for charity plus some fabulous prizes, including a car. And what do you know — Dusty, the stage-struck dustbin has learnt how to talk!

3.15 Battle For The Planet Of The Apes

An exciting feature film in which the world has been devastated by atomic warfare and taken over by intelligent apes. The surviving 'humans' carry out an attack on them.

●★●★●★●★●★●★●●

Christopher
Reeve —
Superman.

Ted Rogers
and his
super Santas.

4.55 Billy Smart's Christmas Circus

Ringmistress Yasmine Smart gets the Greatest Show On Earth off to a cracking start — on horseback with a spectacular troupe of horses. She'll also be bringing into the ring an exotic gathering of acts from all over the world, including death-defying flying trapeze artistes from Mexico.

★●★●★●★●★●★●★●★●●

6.15 The Muppet Show

Danny Kaye is Kermit's special guest in this show but finds he has quite a few problems with the two elderly critics, Waldorf and Statler. He also finds that Miss Piggy is a trifle hostile, to say the least!

Miss Piggy and Kermie her love!

★●★●★●★●★●★●★●★●●

6.45 Diamonds Are Forever

Sean Connery, as James Bond, is sent to Amsterdam to investigate smuggling large quantities of diamonds from South Africa.

9.00 The Morecambe and Wise Christmas Show

Lots of laughs will be dished up with the seasonal turkey and there will also be the traditional partridge in a pear tree — played by a well-known titled person! Many famous people have promised not to appear with Eric and Ern so the only special guest stars will be those who don't mind not being paid.

★●★●★●★ ★●★●★●

Tuesday 26th Dec.

9.00 a.m. Chorlton And The Wheelies

This episode is called **Chorlton And The Snowdragon** in which Fenella's Christmas is spoiled when a hideous new creature arrives in Wheelyworld!

★●★●★●★●★●★●★●★●●

9.25 Get It Together Christmas Special

A sparkling pop extravaganza for Boxing Day introduced by Roy North and Linda Fletcher, with lots of top groups and solo artistes including The Pleasers. The musical backing is provided by Mike Moran and his band and the Teri Scoble Dancers will be adding to the festivities.

10.00 The Ghosts of Motley Hall

The ghosts are preparing for a real old-fashioned Christmas but somehow the spirit just isn't there! It's their task to bring back peace and goodwill to all in the haunted hall. Starring Arthur English, Freddie Jones and Sheila Steafel.

★●★●★●★●★●★●★●★●●

12.00 The Talking Parcel

From the book by Gerald Durrell, this animation fantasy is about a young girl who finds a talking parcel on the sea shore. Inside is a parrot who takes her on a flying train to the beautiful, magical land of Mythologia, where they have all sorts of exciting adventures.

★●★●★●★●★●★●★●★●●

2.10 Holiday On The Buses

Another hilarious romp with those crafty conductors as they once again drive Blakey round the bend! Starring Reg Varney, Bob Grant and Stephen Lewis.

Reg Varney and Stephen Lewis having a break!

Out of this world — that's Sean Connery as James Bond.

3.45 Christmas Star Games

Michael Aspel introduces this special indoor version in which three celebrity teams meet in athletic combat to win £3,000 for children's hospital charities. Amongst others appearing are Linda Thorson, Jackie Pallo, Roger de Courcey, Liza Goddard, Colin Baker and Robin Askwith.

★●★●★●★●★●★●★●

5.30 Charlie's Angels

Another thrilling episode in which the lovely Angels, played by Kate Jackson, Jaclyn Smith and Cheryl Ladd go undercover at a club in Las Vegas. Making a guest appearance as a veteran crooner is Dean Martin.

Wednesday 27th Dec.

12.30 Christmas How

Presenting the programme that never takes itself too seriously are Jack Hargreaves, Jon Miller, Marian Davies and Fred Dinenage. In this special festive programme they'll be showing you how to get your decorations knotted, how to detect the coins in a Xmas pud and even how to drink holly!

L. to r. Jack Hargreaves, Jon Miller, Fred Dinenage and Marian Davies — the team from one of the world's longest-running children's programmes, How.

★●★●★●★●★●★●★●★●★●★●★●★●★●★●

1.30 Pop Quest Christmas Special

Introduced by Mike Read and Sally James, the star contestants include Tim Rice, Jonathan King and Paul Gambaccini.

★●★●★●★●★●★●★●

7.00 George and Mildred

It's a laugh-a-minute when the Ropers and the Fourmiles get together over the Xmas holiday. Goodwill to all men doesn't apply when George and Jeffrey's game of telly-tennis gets out of hand! Starring Yootha Joyce, Brian Murphy, Norman Eshley, Sheila Fearn and Nicholas Bond-Owen.

L. to r. Cheryl Ladd, Jaclyn Smith, Dean Martin, David Doyle and Kate Jackson.

★●★●★●★●★●★●★●★●★●★●★●★●★●★●

7.15 The Benny Hill Show

Benny (below) is back again with the usual collection of crazy characters, including the amazing Professor Marvo, Wild Jack McGrew, and, of course, the indestructible Fred Scuttle. Helping things along are Henry McGee and Jenny Lee Wright.

George (Brian Murphy) gets an earful from Mildred (Yootha Joyce)!

23rd December 1978

THE BIONIC WOMAN™

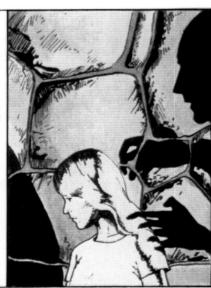

GIVEN A KEY—ONE OF SIX REQUIRED TO OPEN THE MYSTERIOUS VAULT IN THE GRIM AND LONELY HOUSE OF THE SIX LOCKS, ONCE OWNED BY RECLUSE EBENEEZER KANE, JAIME IS PLUNGED INTO A NIGHTMARE! ONE BY ONE, FIVE KANE RELATIVES ARE MURDERED—AND THEN, IN A SECRET PASSAGE SOMEWHERE BENEATH THE STAIRS...

MMMFF!

KEEP AWAY FROM ME, KRAKE! I'M MORE THAN A MATCH FOR YOU—AND YOU'D BETTER BELIEVE IT!

AGONISING SECONDS OF SILENCE... AND NOW THE SCRAPE OF A MATCH...

UUHH! DON'T—DON'T TRY ANYTHING! YOUR LITTLE GAME OF MURDER'S OVER!

JAIME'S RIGHT ELBOW GOES BACK LIKE A PISTON! BUT EVEN AS HER UNSEEN ASSAILANT GASPS WITH PAIN, THE LIGHTS GO OUT!

A FROWN TOUCHES THE SINISTER BUTLER'S GAUNT FACE...

ARE YOU IN TROUBLE, MISS SOMMERS..?

THERE IS NO DEATH ON MY CONSCIENCE, I HAVE BEEN SEARCHING—AND I HAVE FOUND MECHANICAL DEVICES THAT ACCOUNT FOR EVERY KILLING...

SOMETHING IN THE SONOROUS VOICE TELLS JAIME THAT THE MAN ISN'T LYING...

BUT—BUT IF IT WASN'T YOU, THAT ONLY LEAVES...

EXACTLY! KELMAN BREECH—AT YOUR SERVICE! YOU NEVER SUSPECTED THE FAMILY'S FAITHFUL LAWYER, DID YOU? YOU HAD BETTER GIVE ME YOUR KEY MISS SOMMERS!

INSANE GREED BLAZING IN HIS EYES, BREECH LUNGES FORWARD...

AAAGH!

THE KEY!

AS THE BLADE FLASHES AGAIN...

THUDD!

BREECH WILL KILL NO MORE. NOW THE GAME OF MURDER **IS** OVER!

WITH HER OWN KEY, AND THE FIVE SHE TAKES FROM THE SATANIC LAWYER'S POCKET, JAIME FOLLOWS THE BUTLER TO THE MYSTERIOUS VAULT...

DO YOU **KNOW** WHAT'S BEHIND HERE, KRAKE?

NOBODY KNEW SAVE THE LATE MR. EBENEEZER, MISS SOMMERS!

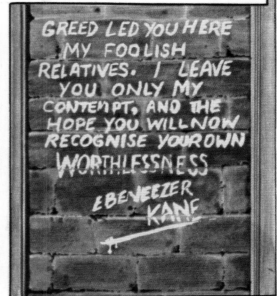

AT LAST, THE LONG-SEALED DOOR GROANS OPEN...

GREED LED YOU HERE MY FOOLISH RELATIVES. I LEAVE YOU ONLY MY CONTEMPT, AND THE HOPE YOU WILL NOW RECOGNISE YOUR OWN WORTHLESSNESS

EBENEEZER KANE

G-GOOD GRIEF!..IT-IT WAS ALL A PRACTICAL JOKE! AND SIX PEOPLE HAVE **DIED** FOR IT!

THAT **WOULD** HAVE AMUSED MY MASTER. HE WAS A STRANGE, UNFATHOMABLE MAN, MISS SOMMERS!

APPALLED, JAIME LOSES NO TIME IN LEAVING THE GHASTLY HOUSE WITH ITS BURDEN OF HORROR...

YOU CAN LEAVE ME TO INFORM THE AUTHORITIES, KRAKE. YOU WON'T COME WITH ME..?

I AM PART OF THIS PLACE, MISS. I HAVE NO FEAR OF STAYING. FAREWELL, FOR I FANCY WE SHALL NEVER MEET AGAIN!

AS IF THE SHADES OF THE DEAD ARE WATCHING HER GO, JAIME BREAKS INTO A RUN...

I'D FACE ANY MISSION OSCAR CARES TO GIVE ME... BUT I COULDN'T TAKE ON THAT EXPERIENCE AGAIN — AS LONG AS I LIVE..!

A great new story starts next week!

29th July 1978

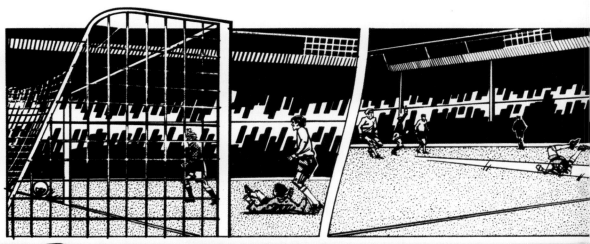

ON THE BALL PRESENTED BY BRIAN MOORE

THE AULD ENEMY

THE highlight of the Home International Tournament is usually the clash between England and Scotland (though I'm sure that the fans that follow the fortunes of Wales and Northern Ireland will be quick to disagree . . .). The confrontation between these two great soccer nations rarely results in a disappointment, on the contrary the outcome of the game can be quite a shock. Take last year; Scotland were then riding high, preparing for their trip to Argentina, England were re-organising themselves under Ron Greenwood. Backed by their fanatical supporters, all the odds pointed to a Scottish victory. Yet, after dominating the game, the Scots lost to England, who snatched a late victory, the winner coming from Steve Coppell.

The year before, it seemed as if the entire population of Scotland had upped camp and migrated to London. You'd have thought Wembley was Hampden, so loud were the chants of the Scottish supporters! England were taken apart that day by a Scotland team that surged forward in full song. Clemence was beaten by Kenny Dalglish and Gordon McQueen in a match that contained all the passion and excitement that one could possibly hope for. Now we're going to go a little farther back in time, in fact to 1967, when England entertained Scotland at Wembley. Could England win, a victory that would take them to an unbeatable margin in the table or could the Scots turn the table? Read on!

In 1967, England came to Wembley World Champions. The side had gone matches without defeat. England had ready defeated Wales by the handso margin of 5-1 and Ireland 2-0. Scotland h beaten Ireland 2-1 and drawn with Wa 1-1. England needed only to draw with Scots to win the Home Championship a few fans gave Scotland any real chance pulling off a shock victory against a vas experienced England.

The England team virtually picked its with the exception of Jimmy Greaves. T immensely gifted striker had once aga found favour with Sir Alf Ramsey and w back in the England side. The man dropp was Liverpool's Roger Hunt. In contrast England's settled formation, Scottish te boss Bobby Brown made no fewer than changes to his side. A major change was inclusion of veteran 'keeper Ronnie Sin son, who, at the age of 36, became the seco oldest Scottish 'keeper ever to make his

Drawn by Sheridon Davies

In the 27th minute of the game, the goal that just had to come for Scotland was popped away by Denis Law (right). Continual Scottish pressure brought their second goal, a super shot from Bobby Lennox (far right).

England had recalled one of the world's most gifted strikers, Jimmy Greaves, (left) for the game. There had been a lot of controversy when Greaves had been relegated in favour of Roger Hunt, for the World Cup the previous summer but Hunt's industrious approach had suited England and he had a fine series of games. Now, however, Hunt was out and Jimmy was back in the England shirt. Sadly for England, Jimmy was never allowed to show what he was capable of and he and Geoff Hurst were shackled for most of the game by a solid Scottish defence.

The Scottish defer was covered well new cap Ronnie Simpson (left). Wl a marvellous seas Simpson had ha with Celtic and n Scotland. His clu had made a clea sweep at home before adding th European Cup to sideboard!

ternational debut. Simpson had starred in the Celtic team that had won the European Cup that very year. However, it was Scotland who began as if they were the world-beaters, launching attack after attack against England. Twelve minutes into the game, central defender Jackie Charlton tackled Lennox, injuring a foot in the process. He left the field later to return in attack, swapping playing roles with his brother Bobby. This injury undoubtedly affected the mobility and understanding of England's defence. It lasted just fifteen minutes. In the 27th minute Jim Baxter took a free-kick on the edge of England's penalty area. Willie Wallace struck a firm shot that was deflected off a defender straight into the path of Denis Law who converted the simplest of chances. Scotland now took complete control. The English attack looked non-existent, the defence terribly shaky under the Scottish pressure.

With just nine minutes of the match remaining, it was Bobby Lennox who drove a right foot shot into the English net to put the Scots two goals in front. Still under the whip, England contrived to stage a recovery and Jackie Charlton pulled one back from a cross by Alan Ball. Scotland surged forward yet again and this time it was another new face, Jim McCalliog, who netted his side's third goal. Incredibly, England pulled another goal back, a Geoff Hurst header from a Bobby Charlton cross. Could the home side score a third? It was not to be and Scotland had pulled off a shock, memorable three-two victory. Four goals had been scored in the final nine minutes of the game. Indeed it was Scotland who took the Home Championship and England had to be content with the runners-up spot. With such a history of upsets whenever England and Scotland play each other you won't catch many people predicting the outcome of this year's meeting. One thing's for sure, it'll be a cracker of a match!

An injured Jackie Charlton (far left) pulled back a goal for England. Brief hopes of an equaliser were soon extinguished when Jim McCalliog (arrowed) hit his first and Scotland's third, past Gordon Banks.

Scotland's answer to Jimmy Greaves was the mercurial Denis Law (right), playing at his peak. He notched away the first goal for Scotland, a simple affair in comparison to the more typical Law efforts, those superbly timed headers, the speed and agility in the goalmouth followed by a telling shot.

To round off a marvellous match, Geoff Hurst (right) climbed high to nod home England's second, just before the final whistle.

SAPPHIRE & STEEL

A SATURDAY AFTERNOON IN THE TENTH FLOOR FLAT OF A SOUTH LONDON HIGH-RISE BLOCK. PETER AND JENNY SIMSON HEAR THE FRONT DOOR OPEN AS THEIR DAUGHTER DIANE COMES IN FROM PLAY...

COME ON, PUSS! THIS WAY, TIGGY!

OH, FOR PETE'S SAKE! SHE HASN'T...

SHE'S BEEN TOLD A MILLION TIMES!

DI! ANOTHER STRAY? YOU KNOW WE'RE NOT ALLOWED PETS HERE!

OH, TIGGY'S DIFFERENT, DAD!

RULES ARE RULES, LOVE!

IT'S ALL RIGHT, TIGGY! YOU'RE MAKE-BELIEVE, AREN'T YOU! THERE'S A GOOD CAT!

STONE ME!

ISN'T HE NICE? ALL BLACK AND WHITE AND CUDDLY!

ER — SMASHING! REAL HANDSOME! LEMME GIVE HIM A STROKE!

COME ON, TIGGY! I'LL INTRODUCE YOU TO YOUR NEW FRIENDS!

THAT CHILD'S IMAGINATION!

MUST GET IT FROM YOU. I NEVER MADE UP THINGS LIKE THAT WHEN I WAS YOUNG.

THAT NIGHT, WHEN DIANE SIMSON GOES TO BED...

CAREFUL, MUM! YOU'RE KNOCKING TIGGY! HE'S CUDDLED UP TO SLEEP WITH ME!

WHY, SO HE IS! SORRY, TIGGY!

THE LIGHTS GO OUT, AND DIANE SLEEPILY MUTTERS A SNATCH OF A POEM...

TIGGY TIGGY, BLACK AND WHITE, GOES A-HUNTING THROUGH THE NIGHT...

AND EVEN AS HER EYES CLOSE...

RROWLLLL...

19th January 1980 • Art:Arthur Ranson • Story:Angus P.Allan

RRRRRR

BALEFUL EYES GLARE ROUND THE EMPTY LIVING ROOM... AND THEN...

KRRASH!

IN THEIR BEDROOM, THE SIMSONS HEAR NOTHING...

...UNTIL THE INSISTENT RINGING OF THE DOOR-BELL PENETRATES!

WHAT THE DICKENS...?

MAY WE COME IN, MR SIMSON? MY NAME'S SAPPHIRE AND THIS IS STEEL. YOU MAY NOT KNOW IT, BUT YOU'RE IN TROUBLE.

IF THIS IS SOME KIND OF MUGGING...

CALM DOWN. WE'RE HERE TO HELP, THAT'S ALL. YOUR DAUGHTER, DIANE...

AT THAT MOMENT, DIANE'S BEDROOM DOOR FLIES FULLY OPEN...

BEGONE! YOU THINK YOU CAN OVERCOME THE POWER OF HECATE? BEGONE— BEFORE YOU SHRIVEL!

More amazing developments on page 136

SUPER FAMOUS FIVE COMPETITION!

This is the bike used by Jenny Thanisch (Anne) in the TV series, which we're offering as a prize.

BICYCLE AND WRIST-WATCHES MUST BE WON!

With **The Famous Five** now on screen again, not only do we look at the show in our super feature (on page 25); we've also arranged a competition with a difference!

As avid viewers of the series will know, The Famous Five love to get on their bikes and ride! Well, you could be the lucky owner of one of our intrepid adventurers' machines — it belonged to Jenny Thanisch, who plays Anne — if you win our exciting competition.

The bike was actually used by Jenny during the last series of **The Famous Five** — that's her standing by it in our photograph — and Southern TV have arranged to have it delivered to the winner's home.

But that's not all. To another four Famous Five fans we're offering the watches worn by the stars of the series. There's Dick's (Gary Russell) 19-jewel Sekonda watch, Anne's (Jenny Thanisch) red-strap Timex, George's (Michelle Gallagher) time-and-date Timex, and Julian's (Marcus Harris) time-and-date Timex. One of these will be sent to each of the four runners-up in the competition.

Remember — the bicycle and the watches were used by the actors and actresses on **The Famous Five** series — so there's every chance that you've already seen our prizes on the TV

screen! But do bear in mind that they're not brand-new, not after all that frantic **Famous Five** action!

WHAT YOU HAVE TO DO: If you're a true Famous Five fan, you really shouldn't have much trouble with this one! Just take a look at the names of popular **Famous Five** books by Enid Blyton, printed on the coupon. In each case, we've left out one of the words and you have to fill in the correct one in the space provided. To assist you, we've printed the words you'll need, in jumbled-up order, of course. When you have completed all the **Famous Five** book titles, add your name, address, and age, attach the coupon firmly to a postcard only, and send it to: Look-in Famous Five Competition, P.O. Box 141, London SE6 3HR, to arrive not later than Monday, July 23rd, 1979. The sender of the first all-correct entry drawn from the postbag after that date will be awarded Jenny Thanisch's bicycle, and the four runners-up will each receive a **Famous Five** watch.

ADVENTURING	**HIKE**
MYSTERY	**SMUGGLER'S**
CAMP	**CARAVAN**
BILLYCOCK	**FINNISTON**
KIRRIN	**TRAIL**

Send, on a postcard only, to:
Look-in Famous Five Competition,
PO Box 141, London SE6 3HR.

FIVE GO TO .... HILL
FIVE GO OFF IN A ....
FIVE GO TO .... MOOR
FIVE ON A .... TOGETHER
FIVE ON A SECRET ....
FIVE ON .... FARM
FIVE GO .... AGAIN
FIVE ON .... ISLAND
FIVE GO OFF TO ....
FIVE GO TO .... TOP

Name ....

Address ....

....

....

.... Age.....

Closing date: Monday, July 23rd, 1979

THE FEATHERED SERPENT
SIMON's WEDDING DAY!

This Monday, Thames TV's The Feathered Serpent features the long-awaited wedding of the beautiful Princess Chimalma (Diane Keen) to Prince Heumac (Brian Deacon). And for one Look-in reader in particular, Simon Theobald, of Bramcote, Notts, it's an extra-special day — for Simon was the winner of our design-a-wedding dress competition, and his entry was made up by Firenze-Peruzzi of Rome into the actual dress that you can see in Monday's episode.

The show's costume designer, Martin Baugh, who was one of the judges of our competition, told us recently: *"Simon's entry was simply the best of the lot, although it took half a day to judge the entries. We had to modify the design slightly because it had to tie in a little more with the contemporary styles of the Aztecs of that period. It was necessary to go to Rome, because they are the best in their field at this sort of design. From start to finish, the actual making of the dress took a fortnight, which included us filming inserts for a feature recently shown on Magpie."*

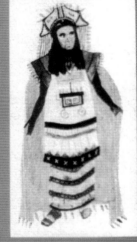

Left: Beautiful Princess Chimalma (Diane Keen) wearing the stunning wedding dress based on the original design (right) by Look-in competition winner Simon Theobald. Below left: The Feathered Serpent costume designer Martin Baugh (left) and Simon Theobald (right) look on as Julia, tailoress for Italian costumiers Peruzzi, starts work on the wedding dress. Below: Martin and Simon discussing the details of the modified version of Simon's winning design.

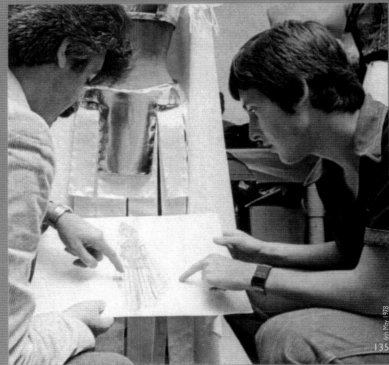

SAPPHIRE & STEEL

DIANE SIMSON, AN ORDINARY GIRL LIVING IN AN ORDINARY HIGH-RISE FLAT, IMAGINES HERSELF OWNING A PET CAT... BUT IMAGINATION BECOMES REALITY! LATE AT NIGHT, SAPPHIRE AND STEEL ARRIVE TO FIND THE CHILD TRANSFORMED!

BEGONE! YOU SHALL NOT OVER COME THE SPIRIT OF HECATE!

ALL IS CHAOS! HER MOTHER FALLS IN A FAINT, HER FATHER IS PARALYSED WITH FEAR! NOW THE SHRIEKING VOICE CALLS HER CAT FROM THE RUIN OF THE LIVING ROOM!

NEXT INSTANT, AS THOUGH BEATEN BACK BY A BLAST OF TANGIBLE EVIL...

ASIDE, YOU FOOLS! NONE STANDS AGAINST HECATE!

NNUGGH!

NROWWLLL!

COME, GRIMALKIN! LET US FULFIL OUR DESTINY!

AS THOUGH STRICKEN IMMOBILE, SAPPHIRE AND STEEL ARE HELPLESS TO FOLLOW! BUT THE SPELL—AND SPELL IT IS—WEARS OFF...

LOOK AFTER THEM, STEEL!

SAPPHIRE GOES INTO DIANE'S BEDROOM...

AS I EXPECTED. CATALEPTIC. TO ALL INTENTS AND PURPOSES— DEAD!

NOTHING CAN ROUSE THE GIRL. AFTER SAPPHIRE EXAMINES THE ROOM...

THE ROOM! IT'S — IT'S DEMOLISHED! AS IF BY THAT CAT... BUT THERE WAS NO CAT!

OH YES THERE WAS, MR. SIMSON. THE ONE YOUR DAUGHTER BROUGHT FROM THE DEPTHS OF TIME, PERHAPS BY SOME TRIGGER— SOME PHRASE SHE SAID...

26th January 1980

WHAT ARE YOU **SAYING**? WHAT'S **HAPPENED** TO DIANE?

YOU CAN'T HELP HER. SHE'S RELEASED A POWER OF EVIL, FROM THE PAST. IT'S APPEARED IN THE SHAPE OF THAT ANIMAL, AND IT'S **CLAIMED** HER...

HECATE. SHE SAID SHE WAS **HECATE**. THE GREATEST WITCH OF ANCIENT TIMES. WHAT HAVOC SHE COULD CREATE IN THIS AGE, WITH HER SATANIC FAMILIAR...

I WANT MY D-DIANE BACK! I WANT TO STOP THIS N-NIGHTMARE!

WE'LL DO WHAT WE CAN, MRS. SIMSON. YOUR DAUGHTER SLEEPS. LET'S HOPE THAT STEEL AND I WILL HAVE THE POWER TO **WAKEN** HER AGAIN...

MEANWHILE...

COME, GRIMALKIN! NOW LET US **TEST** OUR POWERS! SHALL DESTRUCTION FLOW FROM MY FINGERTIPS AS IT DID OF OLD..?

NYAH-HAAH HAAH **HAHH**! EXCELLENT! SPLENDID! WHAT **MISCHIEF** WE CAN MAKE HERE IN THIS MODERN WORLD!

AS THE NIGHT SHRILLS TO ALARM, AND THE BLAZE OF THE RUINED POWER-STATION PAINTS THE SKY A LURID RED...

HOW CAN WE STOP HER? WE DON'T KNOW WHERE SHE'S GONE!

WE HAVE TO FIND HER, STEEL. NEVER MIND THIS CITY— A LITTLE **GIRL'S** LIFE DEPENDS ON IT...

137

26th January 1980

Can they save her? Find out on page 140

THE Boomtown RATS

Brainy Smurf

The MUPPET SHOW

I'M DESPERATE FOR YOU

When in doubt PANIC

SUPERMAN

SPACE CRUISER

Keep on Truckin'...

I'm lookin good!

MICKEY MOUSE CLUB

ELVIS COSTELLO

NICE ONE!

Here's just a tiny selection of the badges around at the moment — and you can draw your own in the blank space (below).

HAVE A HAPPY DAY

tomorrow we must get organised

Spring Fitv

ONLY ROTTERS HUNT OTTERS

BORED TEENAGER was the big seller a couple of years ago, probably because it summed up a punk generation's attitude to life, while the best seller in London last winter was **I used to be uncertain, now I'm not so sure.**

Pop and rock fans are in luck, of course, as record companies often issue thousands of free badges to promote their new releases. Film companies sometimes do the same, except if it's a very successful movie, in which case they *charge* for badges; so you are paying for the privilege of being a walking advertisement.

The first big badge bonanza started almost 20 years ago with the heyday of Elvis Presley. His manager Colonel Parker hit on the idea of selling badges with his picture and **I Love You Elvis** on them. They sold in hundreds of thousands to swooning girl fans. Then the crafty Colonel doubled his money, by selling thousands more to their boyfriends emblazoned with **I Hate You Elvis**, which helped them get over their jealousy. Sadly, there was another boom in Elvis badges not long ago, with the message **The King Is Dead.**

Sadly in a different way was the fortune one badge maker hoped to make when Scotland qualified for the World Cup finals in Argentina. Based on the **Evita** hit, **We'll Make You Cry Argentina** was worn proudly by thousands of Scots fans before their team was bounced out of the competition. From then on, you couldn't see a single badge of that description from John O'Groats to Berwick.

Badges were first popular here as decorative items at the turn of the century, mostly with pictures of the King and Queen and with loyal messages like **Rule Britannia** and **England's Empire On Which The Sun Never Sets.** The basic design of the badge has hardly changed since then, except for the safety clip. I don't think you can say that about any other current fashion.

Nowadays badges are used for all kinds of causes. In ecology, one of the best was the anti-nuclear power motto: **Windscale — It Will Cost The Earth.** Another

successful badge slogan which may have helped make the otter a Protected Species last year was **Only Rotters Hunt Otters.**

That reminds me of the sex war that is waged on people's lapels. There were a couple of Women's Lib badges imported not long ago from America, reading **A Woman Needs A Man Like A Moose**

STEWPOT INVESTIGATES . . .

Every day more and more people are getting stuck on badges. The craze is catching up in popularity on t-shirts all the time. One reason is that badges are cheaper, from about 5p up to £2 for a really elaborate one. You can wear them with everything and they come in all categories, from punk to politics, from ecology to sport, from pictures of pop and TV idols to funny sayings. You name it, there's a badge to cover it!

Needs A Hat Rack and **A Woman Needs A Man Like A Fish Needs A Bicycle.** But the chaps were quick to fire back, with **A Man Without A Woman Is Like A Neck Without A Pain.**

America is where it all started, which is true of so many zany fashions. In fact over two centuries ago they produced a badge worn proudly on the jackets of the country's proud citizens in the shape of an eagle — the American emblem. It was at first going to be a turkey, but Benjamin Franklin didn't like the look of that wrinkled head, or its short-tempered character.

Badges can have very practical uses. Apart from expressing your political views, plugging your product and worshipping your idols, they can also help you make friends. Back to the USA again, where they have badges called **Hi-Signs** which say **You are Cute — Wanna Say Hello?, R U Attached?** and even **Take Me, I'm Yours.** They are shaped like large lollipops and are said to be great for starting new relationships — when accompanied by large smiles . . .

There is a unique basement showroom in London's Covent Garden called **The Badge**

Shop run by 27-years-old badge enthusiast Des Kay.

"They are an expression of your personality, or give you a feeling of belonging to a particular movement or attitude to life," said Des. Among his long-term big sellers, originating from America, are **Nice One** and **Keep On Trucking.** And then there are the clever 'philosophical' slogans like **I Think. Therefore I am. (I think).** And **Tomorrow We Must Get Organised.**

His shop, at 45 Monmouth Street, London, W.C.2 is often jam-packed with foreign tourists. London is usually brimming with overseas visitors anyway, and I wonder what they think when they see his best selling **I'm NOT A Tourist — I Live Here.**

Should any overseas customer get upset with the idea that his kind aren't welcome and start trouble, the advice for nervous customers is on another badge stating **When In Doubt — PANIC!!!.** It is stuck up in a showcase next to another of my favourites, which says **We Are The People Our Parents Warned Us Against.**

"Punk and The New Wave has certainly given the business a shot in the arm not to mention a prick in the chest," said one manufacturer. "The longer they want to cover their arms, legs, belts, shoulders and backs with badges, the more need there is for better, cleverer, more striking designs." There's even more demand now from older people wanting to express an opinion — from advising you to **Smile** to wanting to change the government!"

My opinion is that though I'm not wild about walking pin-cushions, I like the witty, well-designed badges. They are fun and they are friendly, (although I wonder if the one saying **Help!! I'm A Prisoner In A**

Badge Factory *was* just a joke . . ?) And if all this has whetted your appetite, you can have a go at designing your very own badge slogan on the opposite page.

SAPPHIRE & STEEL

AN EVIL FORCE OF TIME PAST, THE LEGENDARY WITCH NAMED HECATE HAS FORCED, WITH HER SATANIC CAT, GRIMALKIN, HER WAY INTO THE PRESENT THROUGH THE VIVID IMAGINATION OF A LITTLE GIRL, DIANE SIMSON. WHILE DIANE LIES IN A DEATH-LIKE COMA, SAPPHIRE AND STEEL SET OUT TO COMBAT THE AWFUL POWER, ALREADY EMBARKED ON A TRAIL OF DESTRUCTION...

ONE WAVE OF HER HAND, AND SHE DID **THAT**!

IF WE'RE GOING TO RETURN HER TO THE PAST, WE'VE GOT TO TRAP HER FIRST. BUT HOW, STEEL? **HOW**?

SUDDENLY...

THE CAT! **HER** CAT! SHE SENT IT BACK AGAINST **US**!

STEADY! DON'T LOOK AT ITS EYES. STAY **ABSOLUTELY** STILL!

USING HER POWERS, SAPPHIRE FREEZES TIME FOR ONE PRECIOUS MOMENT... AND CAUGHT IN THE PRESENT, THE ANIMAL IS LOCKED IMMOBILE...

SMOTHER IT, STEEL! **GATHER IT UP**!

I'VE GOT YOU!

NOW THE SNARLING BUNDLE IS SMOTHERED IN STEEL'S JACKET...

COME ON! DIANE SIMSON STARTED THIS — ONLY **SHE** CAN FINISH IT!

THE QUICKER THE BETTER! THE THING'S CLAWING ME TO BITS THROUGH THE MATERIAL!

THE FLAT, WHERE THE SIMSONS ARE KEEPING ENDLESS VIGIL BY THEIR COMATOSE DAUGHTER'S BEDSIDE...

WHA..?

GIVE US ROOM! THIS IS **VITALLY** URGENT!

HEAR ME, DIANE! I'M GOING TO TURN TIME BACK! I'M GOING TO SHOW YOU THE CAT. **YOUR** CAT! BUT YOU WILL REFUSE TO SEE IT. YOU UNDERSTAND? **IT WON'T BE THERE**!

MEANWHILE, DIANE'S OTHER BEING, THE WITCH CALLED HECATE, SENSES THAT SOMETHING IS WRONG!

DO THEY SEEK TO PREVENT MY DESTROYING THIS PLACE? THE FOOLS! I SHALL BEAT THEM YET!

2nd February 1980

A strange new story starts next week.

lookin on your ITV programmes this week:

ANGLIA

SATURDAY
- 10.30 Saturday Banana
- 12.30 World Of Sport
- 5.30 Mork And Mindy
- 6.00 Film
- 8.15 Search For A Star

SUNDAY
- 12.10 Grizzly Adams Xmas Special
- 2.30 The Big Match
- 5.30 Quest Of Eagles
- 7.15 Christmas Glums
- 7.45 Pam Ayres' Canadian Xmas

MONDAY
- 12.30 Christmas Runaround
- 1.30 Ben Hur
- 6.05 You're Only Young Twice
- 7.00 Give Us A Clue
- 8.00 London Night Out

TUESDAY
- 11.00 Lassie
- 2.00 Star Games Final
- 3.05 The James Bond Film
- 6.15 George And Mildred
- 6.45 The Three Musketeers

WEDNESDAY
- 11.00 Scalawag
- 12.45 Cinderella
- 2.00 The King And I
- 4.15 Billy Smart's Xmas Circus
- 6.15 Charlie's Angels

THURSDAY
- 3.00 Charley's Aunt
- 4.15 Clapperboard
- 4.45 Best Gymnasts In The World
- 6.45 Film
- 8.30 Robin's Nest Xmas Special

FRIDAY
- 3.45 Aladdin
- 4.45 Magpie
- 5.15 All-Time Great Top Twenty
- 7.00 The Muppet Show
- 8.00 Film

BORDER

SATURDAY
- 10.30 Tiswas
- 12.30 World Of Sport
- 5.30 Happy Days
- 6.00 Film
- 8.15 Search For A Star

SUNDAY
- 12.10 Grizzly Adams Xmas Special
- 2.30 The Big Match
- 5.30 Quest Of Eagles
- 7.15 Christmas Glums
- 7.45 Pam Ayres' Canadian Xmas

MONDAY
- 12.30 Christmas Runaround
- 1.30 Ben Hur
- 6.05 You're Only Young Twice
- 7.00 Give Us A Clue
- 8.00 London Night Out

TUESDAY
- 11.00 Lassie
- 2.00 Star Games Final
- 3.05 The James Bond Film
- 6.15 George And Mildred
- 6.45 The Three Musketeers

WEDNESDAY
- 11.00 Scalawag
- 12.45 Cinderella
- 2.00 The King And I
- 4.15 Billy Smart's Xmas Circus
- 6.15 Charlie's Angels

THURSDAY
- 3.00 Charley's Aunt
- 4.15 Clapperboard
- 4.45 Best Gymnasts In The World
- 6.45 Film
- 8.30 Robin's Nest Xmas Special

FRIDAY
- 3.45 Aladdin
- 4.45 Magpie
- 5.15 All-Time Great Top Twenty
- 7.00 The Muppet Show
- 8.00 Film

CHANNEL

SATURDAY
- 12.30 World Of Sport
- 5.30 Mork And Mindy
- 6.00 Film
- 7.40 Xmas Sale Of The Century
- 8.15 Search For A Star

SUNDAY
- 2.30 The Big Match
- 3.45 Sunday Matinee
- 5.30 Quest Of Eagles
- 7.15 Christmas Glums
- 7.45 Pam Ayres' Canadian Xmas

MONDAY
- 12.30 Christmas Runaround
- 1.30 Ben Hur
- 5.30 You're Only Young Twice
- 7.00 Give Us A Clue
- 8.00 London Night Out

TUESDAY
- 11.00 Lassie
- 2.00 Star Games Final
- 3.05 The James Bond Film
- 6.15 George And Mildred
- 6.45 The Three Musketeers

WEDNESDAY
- 12.45 Cinderella
- 2.00 The King And I
- 4.15 Billy Smart's Xmas Circus
- 5.45 Winner Takes All
- 6.15 Charlie's Angels

THURSDAY
- 3.00 Charlie's Aunt
- 4.15 Clapperboard
- 4.45 Best Gymnasts In The World
- 6.45 Film
- 8.30 Robin's Nest Xmas Special

FRIDAY
- 3.45 Aladdin
- 4.45 Magpie
- 5.15 All-Time Great Top Twenty
- 7.00 The Muppet Show
- 8.00 Film

GRAMPIAN

SATURDAY
- 10.30 Tiswas
- 12.30 World Of Sport
- 5.30 Happy Days
- 6.00 Film
- 8.15 Search For A Star

SUNDAY
- 12.10 Grizzly Adams Xmas Special
- 4.30 Scotsport
- 5.30 Quest Of Eagles
- 7.15 Christmas Glums
- 7.45 Pam Ayres' Canadian Xmas

MONDAY
- 9.30 Walt Disney Classics
- 12.30 Christmas Runaround
- 1.30 Ben Hur
- 6.05 You're Only Young Twice
- 7.00 London Night Out

TUESDAY
- 11.00 Lassie
- 2.00 Star Games Final
- 3.05 The James Bond Film
- 6.15 George And Mildred
- 6.45 The Three Musketeers

WEDNESDAY
- 11.00 Scalawag
- 12.45 Cinderella
- 2.00 The King And I
- 4.15 Billy Smart's Xmas Circus
- 6.15 Charlie's Angels

THURSDAY
- 3.00 Charley's Aunt
- 4.15 Clapperboard
- 4.45 Best Gynasts In The World
- 6.45 Film
- 8.30 Robin's Next Xmas Special

FRIDAY
- 3.45 Aladdin
- 4.45 Magpie
- 6.30 Sportscall
- 7.00 The Muppet Show
- 8.00 Film

GRANADA

SATURDAY
- 10.30 Tiswas
- 12.30 World Of Sport
- 5.30 Happy Days
- 6.00 Film
- 8.15 Search For A Star

SUNDAY
- 12.10 Grizzly Adams Xmas Special
- 2.30 Kick Off Match
- 5.30 Quest Of Eagles
- 7.15 Christmas Glums
- 7.45 Pam Ayres' Canadian Xmas

MONDAY
- 12.30 Christmas Runaround
- 1.30 Ben Hur
- 6.05 You're Only Young Twice
- 7.00 Give Us A Clue
- 8.00 London Night Out

TUESDAY
- 11.00 Lassie
- 2.00 Star Games Final
- 3.05 The James Bond Film
- 6.15 George And Mildred
- 6.45 The Three Musketeers

WEDNESDAY
- 11.00 Scalawag
- 12.45 Cinderella
- 2.00 The King And I
- 4.15 Billy Smart's Xmas Circus
- 6.15 Charlie's Angels

THURSDAY
- 3.00 Charley's Aunt
- 4.15 Clapperboard
- 4.45 Best Gymnasts In The World
- 6.50 Film
- 8.30 Robin's Nest Xmas Special

FRIDAY
- 3.45 Aladdin
- 4.45 Magpie
- 5.15 All-Time Great Top Twenty
- 7.00 The Muppet Show
- 8.00 Film

MIDLANDS

SATURDAY
- 10.30 Tiswas
- 12.30 World Of Sport
- 5.30 Mork And Mindy
- 6.00 Film
- 8.15 Search For A Star

SUNDAY
- 12.00 Grizzly Adams Xmas Special
- 2.30 Star Soccer
- 5.30 Quest Of Eagles
- 7.15 Christmas Glums
- 7.45 Pam Ayres' Canadian Xmas

MONDAY
- 12.30 Christmas Runaround
- 1.30 Ben Hur
- 6.05 You're Only Young Twice
- 7.00 Give Us A Clue
- 8.00 London Night Out

TUESDAY
- 11.00 Lassie
- 2.00 Star Games Final
- 3.05 The James Bond Film
- 6.15 George And Mildred
- 6.45 The Three Musketeers

WEDNESDAY
- 11.00 Scalawag
- 12.45 Cinderella
- 2.00 The King And I
- 4.45 Billy Smart's Xmas Circus
- 6.15 Charlie's Angels

THURSDAY
- 3.00 Charley's Aunt
- 4.15 Clapperboad
- 4.45 Best Gymnasts In The World
- 6.45 Film
- 8.30 Robin's Nest Xmas Special

FRIDAY
- 3.45 Aladdin
- 4.45 Magpie
- 5.15 All-Time Great Top Twenty
- 7.00 The Muppet Show
- 8.00 Feature Film

SCOTTISH

SATURDAY
- 10.30 Tiswas
- 12.30 World Of Sport
- 5.30 Film
- 7.40 Xmas Sale Of The Century
- 8.15 Search For A Star

SUNDAY
- 12.10 Grizzly Adams Xmas Special
- 4.35 Scotsport
- 5.30 Quest Of Eagles
- 7.15 Christmas Glums
- 7.45 Pam Ayres' Canadian Xmas

MONDAY
- 12.30 Christmas Runaround
- 1.30 Ben Hur
- 5.30 You'r Only Young Twice
- 7.00 Give Us A Clue
- 8.00 London Night Out

TUESDAY
- 11.00 Flintsones Christmas
- 2.00 Star Games Final
- 3.05 The James Bond Film
- 6.15 George And Mildred
- 6.45 The Three Musketeers

WEDNESDAY
- 11.00 Scalawag
- 12.45 Cinderella
- 2.00 The King And I
- 4.15 Billy Smart's Xmas Circus
- 6.15 Charlie's Angels

THURSDAY
- 3.00 Charley's Aunt
- 4.15 Clapperboard
- 4.45 Best Gymnasts In The World
- 6.45 Film
- 8.30 Robin's Nest Xmas Special

FRIDAY
- 3.45 Aladdin
- 4.45 Magpie
- 5.15 All-Time Great Top Twenty
- 7.00 The Muppet Show
- 8.00 Film

SOUTHERN

SATURDAY
- 10.30 Saturday Banana
- 12.30 World Of Sport
- 5.30 Happy Days
- 6.00 Film
- 8.15 Search For A Star

SUNDAY
- 12.10 Grizzly Adams Xmas Special
- 2.30 The Big Match
- 5.30 Quest Of Eagles
- 7.15 Christmas Glums
- 7.45 Pam Ayres' Canadian Xmas

MONDAY
- 9.30 Walt Disney Classics
- 12.30 Christmas Runaround
- 1.30 Ben Hur
- 7.00 Give Us A Clue
- 8.00 London Night Out

TUESDAY
- 11.00 Lassie
- 2.00 Star Games Final
- 3.05 The James Bond Film
- 6.15 George And Mildred
- 6.45 The Three Musketeers

WEDNESDAY
- 11.00 Scalawag
- 12.45 Cinderella
- 2.00 The King And I
- 4.15 Billy Smart's Xmas Circus
- 6.15 Charlie's Angels

THURSDAY
- 3.00 Charley's Aunt
- 4.15 Clapperboard
- 4.45 Best Gymnasts In The World
- 6.45 Film
- 8.30 Robin's Nest Xmas Special

FRIDAY
- 3.45 Aladdin
- 4.45 Magpie
- 5.15 All-Time Great Top Twenty
- 7.00 The Muppet Show
- 8.00 Film

TYNE TEES

SATURDAY
- 9.00 Saturday Shake-up
- 12.30 World Of Sport
- 5.30 Happy Days
- 6.00 Film
- 8.15 Search For A Star

SUNDAY
- 12.10 Grizzly Adams Xmas Special
- 2.30 Shoot!
- 5.30 Quest Of Eagles
- 7.15 Christmas Glums
- 7.45 Pam Ayres' Canadian Xmas

MONDAY
- 12.30 Christmas Runaround
- 1.30 Ben Hur
- 6.05 You're Only Young Twice
- 7.00 Give Us A Clue
- 8.00 London Night Out

TUESDAY
- 11.00 Lassie
- 2.00 Star Games Final
- 3.05 The James Bond Film
- 6.15 George And Mildred
- 6.45 The Three Musketeers

WEDNESDAY
- 11.00 Scalawag
- 12.45 Cinderella
- 2.00 The King And I
- 4.15 Billy Smart's Xmas Circus
- 6.15 Charlie's Angels

THURSDAY
- 3.00 Charley's Aunt
- 4.15 Clapperboard
- 4.45 Best Gymnasts In The World
- 6.45 Film
- 8.30 Robin's Nest Xmas Special

FRIDAY
- 3.45 Aladdin
- 4.45 Magpie
- 5.15 All-Time Great Top Twenty
- 6.25 Sportstime
- 7.00 The Muppet Show

ULSTER

SATURDAY
- 11.30 Christmas In Sesame Street
- 12.30 World of Sport
- 5.30 Mork And Mindy
- 6.00 Film
- 8.15 Search For A Star

SUNDAY
- 12.30 Grizzly Adams Xmas Special
- 2.30 The Big Match
- 5.30 Quest Of Eagles
- 7.15 Christmas Glums
- 7.45 Pam Ayres' Canadian Xmas

MONDAY
- 12.30 Christmas Runaround
- 1.30 Ben Hur
- 6.05 You're Only Young Twice
- 7.00 Give Us A Clue
- 8.00 London Night Out

TUESDAY
- 11.00 Lassie
- 2.00 Star Games Final
- 3.10 The James Bond Film
- 6.15 George And Mildred
- 6.45 The Three Musketeers

WEDNESDAY
- 11.00 Scalawag
- 12.45 Cinderella
- 2.00 The King And I
- 4.15 Billy Smart's Xmas Circus
- 6.15 Charlie's Angels

THURSDAY
- 3.00 Charley's Aunt
- 4.15 Clapperboard
- 4.45 Best Gymnasts In The World
- 6.45 Film
- 8.30 Robin's Nest Xmas Special

FRIDAY
- 3.45 Aladdin
- 4.45 Magpie
- 5.15 All-Time Great Top Twenty
- 6.05 Mary Tyler Moore
- 7.00 The Muppet Show

HTV

SATURDAY
10.30 Tiswas
12.30 World Of Sport
5.30 Mork And Mindy
6.00 Film
8.15 Search For A Star

SUNDAY
12.10 Grizzly Adams Xmas Special
2.30 The Big Match
5.30 Quest Of Eagles
7.15 Christmas Glums
7.45 Pam Ayres' Canadian Xmas

MONDAY
9.30 Walt Disney Classics
12.30 Christmas Runaround
1.30 Ben Hur
7.00 Give Us A Clue
8.30 London Night Out

TUESDAY
11.00 Lassie
2.00 Star Games Final
3.05 The James Bond Film
6.15 George And Mildred
6.45 The Three Musketeers

WEDNESDAY
11.00 Scalawag
12.45 Cinderella
2.00 The King And I
4.15 Billy Smart's Circus
6.15 Charlie's Angels

THURSDAY
3.00 Charley's Aunt
4.15 Clapperboard
4.45 Best Gymnasts In The World
6.45 Film
8.30 Robin's Nest Xmas Special

FRIDAY
3.45 Aladdin
4.45 Magpie
5.15 All-Time Great TOp Twenty
7.00 The Muppet Show
8.00 Film

LWT/THAMES

THAMES

SATURDAY
10.30 Tiswas
12.30 World Of Sport
5.30 Happy Days
6.00 Film
8.15 Search For A Star

SUNDAY
12.10 Grizzly Adams Xmas Special
2.30 The Big Match
5.30 Quest Of Eagles
7.15 Christmas Glums
7.45 Pam Ayres' Canadian Xmas

MONDAY
12.30 Christmas Runaround
1.30 Ben Hur
6.05 You're Only Young Twice
7.00 Give Us A Clue
8.00 London Night Out

TUESDAY
11.00 Lassie
2.00 Star Games Final
3.05 The James Bond Film
6.15 George And Mildred
6.45 The Three Musketeers

WEDNESDAY
11.00 Scalawag
12.45 Cinderella
2.00 The King And I
4.15 Billy Smart's Xmas Circus
6.15 Charlie's Angels

THURSDAY
3.00 Charley's Aunt
4.15 Christmas Clapperboard
4.45 Best Gymnasts In The World
6.45 Film
8.30 Robin's Nest Xmas Special

FRIDAY
3.45 Aladdin
4.45 Magpie
5.15 All-Time Great Top Twenty
7.00 The Muppet Show
8.00 Film

WESTWARD

SATURDAY
9.20 Morning Picture Show
12.30 World Of Sport
5.30 Mork And Mindy
6.00 Film
8.15 Search For A Star

SUNDAY
12.10 Grizzly Adams Xmas Special
2.30 The Big Match
5.30 Quest Of Eagles
7.15 Christmas Glums
7.45 Pam Ayres' Canadian Xmas

MONDAY
12.30 Christmas Runaround
1.30 Ben Hur
5.30 You're Only Young Twice
7.00 Give Us A Clue
8.00 London Night Out

TUESDAY
11.00 Lassie
2.00 Star Games Final
3.05 The James Bond Film
6.15 George And Mildred
6.45 The Three Musketeers

WEDNESDAY
11.00 Scalawag
12.45 Cinderella
2.00 The King And I
4.15 Billy Smart's Xmas Circus
6.15 Charlie's Angels

THURSDAY
3.00 Charley's Aunt
4.15 Clapperboard
4.45 Best Gynasts In The World
6.45 Film
8.30 Robin's Nest Xmas Special

FRIDAY
3.45 Aladdin
4.45 Magpie
5.15 All-Time Great Top Twenty
7.00 The Muppet Show
8.00 Film

YORKSHIRE

SATURDAY
10.30 Tiswas
12.30 World Of Sport
5.30 Happy Days
6.00 Film
8.15 Search For A Star

SUNDAY
12.10 Grizzly Adams Xmas Special
2.30 Football Special
5.30 Quest Of Eagles
7.15 Christmas Glums
7.45 Pam Ayres' Canadian Xmas

MONDAY
12.30 Christmas Runaround
1.30 Ben Hur
6.05 You're Only Young Twice
7.00 Give Us A Clue
8.00 London Night Out

TUESDAY
11.00 Lassie
2.00 Star Games Final
3.05 The James Bond Film
6.45 George And Mildred
6.45 The Three Musketeers

WEDNESDAY
11.00 Scalawag
12.45 Cinderella
2.00 The King And I
4.45 Billy Smart's Xmas Circus
6.15 Charlie's Angels

THURSDAY
3.00 Charley's Aunt
4.15 Clapperboard
4.45 Best Gymnasts In The World
6.45 Film
8.30 Robin's Nest Xmas Special

FRIDAY
3.45 Aladdin
4.45 Magpie
5.15 All-Time Great Top Twenty
7.00 The Muppet Show
8.00 Film

Racey

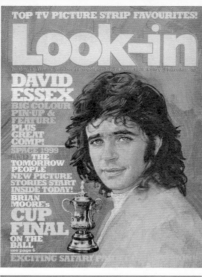
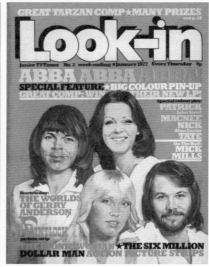

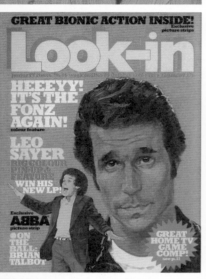
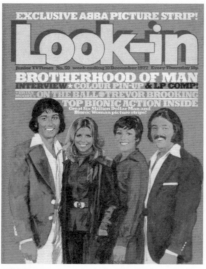

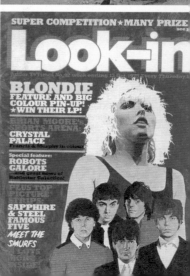